MANAGING HUMAN RESOURCES
IN THE HUMAN SERVICES

MANAGING HUMAN RESOURCES IN THE HUMAN SERVICES
Supervisory Challenges

Felice Davidson Perlmutter
Temple University

Darlyne Bailey
Case Western Reserve University

F. Ellen Netting
Virginia Commonwealth University

New York   Oxford
OXFORD UNIVERSITY PRESS
2001

Oxford University Press

Oxford   New York
Athens   Auckland   Bangkok   Bogotá   Buenos Aires   Calcutta
Cape Town   Chennai   Dar es Salaam   Delhi   Florence   Hong Kong   Istanbul
Karachi   Kuala Lumpur   Madrid   Melbourne   Mexico City   Mumbai
Nairobi   Paris   São Paulo   Singapore   Taipei   Tokyo   Toronto   Warsaw

and associated companies
Berlin   Ibadan

Copyright © 2001 by Oxford University Press

Published by Oxford University Press, Inc.,
198 Madison Avenue, New York, New York, 10016
http://www.oup-usa.org

Oxford is a registered trademark of Oxford University Press.

Library of Congress Cataloging-in-Publication Data
Perlmutter, Felice Davidson
    Managing human resources in the human services : supervisory
challenges / Felice Davidson Perlmutter, Darlyne Bailey, F. Ellen
Netting. p. cm.
    Includes bibliographical references and index.
    ISBN 0-19-513707-8 (pb. : alk. paper). — ISBN 0-19-512027-2 (cl.
: alk. paper)
    1. Human services personnel—Supervision of—United States.
2. Personnel management—United States. I. Bailey, Darlyne.
II. Netting, F. Ellen. III. Title.
HV40.54.P39 2000
658.3—dc21   99-39955
                                                                           CIP

Printing (last digit): 10 9 8 7 6 5 4 3 2 1

Printed in the United States of America
on acid-free paper

This book is dedicated to the committed managerial supervisors whose critical roles in this period of social and political upheaval make them the unsung heroes and heroines of the human services.

Contents

Foreword

Managing Human Resources in the Human Services: Supervisory Challenges is a book that begins to fill a huge gap in the nonprofit organizational literature. Each of the authors of this book is well known for her work in human service management. Working together—a nice human resources model—they have produced a usable, student- and employee-friendly, hands-on book that will resonate with human service executives. In particular, it addresses the many needs of the middle managers in the human service field—assistant and associate directors, for example—on whom the brunt of the human resources function falls and for whom we have done little. And it will serve well in classes on human resources in the human service enterprise.

The organization of the book is excellent. The first part deals with legal issues, strategic basics such as communication, diversity, compensation, performance appraisal, motivation, working with teams, and the thorny issue of evaluation.

The chapters throughout are user friendly both in structure and in attention to human service and social work concerns. The authors know where the reader is coming from! The chapters present key dilemmas that must be addressed at the agency level and case material that helps all readers obtain a realistic grasp of the material.

One of the most interesting chapters is that on "Protecting Managers as Workers." This is important and appropriate because most human resources texts forget that the manager *is* an employee with the same kinds of concerns and issues that other employees have, and in an important sense, fewer resources to deal with them.

Another pathbreaking chapter, "Motivating, Appraising, and Rewarding," deals with the issue of compensation, of critical concern since human service agencies have to address this vital issue. I am thinking not only of the amount of compensation that needs to be increased, but also the distribution of limited funds and resources in the agency. More performance-based compensation is needed.

Amazingly we have few books on human resources management in the human services. This book, one with human services cases, has a human service perspective and human service soul. It creates an immediate connection with both professionals in the field and with students preparing for administrative positions.

In today's environment, the not-for-profit human services enterprise is no longer "entitled" to do the work it has done because "it is good work." All too often, executives drift into their jobs with little prior preparation, struggle to do the best they can, get little support, and struggle some more. Frequently, excellence at clinical work is the criterion of choice with little regard for whether the worker has any managerial ability. The clinician turned executive, applying clinical skills and methods to managerial problems, is an all too familiar sign in the human service agency. In sum, borrowing from the words of W. S. Gilbert, "The nonprofit manager's lot is not a happy one." And I would go further—I think the sector as a whole has suffered from this lacuna.

Happily, "the times, they are a-changin'." Programs in human service administration are now developing. Many books are being written on nonprofit management, administration, and leadership. And, even better, materials on managerial components—including human resources management and supervision—are surfacing. This book is a fine example!

The materials in this excellent volume in part address this shameful legacy. For one thing the book clearly sets out the staff as a major resource, and indicates that the staff needs to be managed through a human resources perspective. An enriched staff and happy staff is a more productive one. That staff human resources need to be managed proactively is one of this book's important messages. It should be human services agencies, not commercial ones, that are in the forefront of the "family-friendly" movement.

High quality human resources are an essential element in achieving peak performance agencies. This book makes a wonderful start on this journey, and will be a useful companion for agency directors and students alike. Use it in good organizational health!

John Tropman, Professor
University of Michigan

Preface

Managerial supervisors play a central role in the human services as they interface with upper level management and with the front line workers they supervise (Perlmutter, 1983). They connect the work within the culture of bureaucracy and the culture of service provision (Holloway & Brager, 1989).

We view managerial supervisors as professionals whose distinguishing characteristic is their oversight, evaluation, and responsibility for the work performance and accountability of their supervisees. Managerial supervisors are found at all levels throughout the human service agency.

Consequently the assumption that underpins this book is that managerial supervisors have unique roles to play in the delivery of effective and efficient services to clients and consumers. We believe that their work must be recognized and supported.

Professionals who have chosen these careers have, to a large extent, been motivated by their social awareness and concern for those in need. The importance of the work being performed, and the importance of its effect on people's lives, requires not only a sense of confidence in the valuable contributions being made by their organizations but also a sense of competency in their own professional performance.

Yet there is a basic paradox inherent in this situation. Managerial supervisors have often moved up the hierarchy as a result of their professional competence in working directly with clients and consumers, but their new positions require a different set of skills—administrative skills. Consequently managerial supervisors are often ill prepared for these managerial demands and expectatations and feel uncomfortable in their administrative positions. There exists a fundamental gap in their preparedness, which is often the cause of great anxiety and tension.

In spite of this need that results from a change in role, supervisory level managers do not always receive from their superiors adequate supervision or mentorship in the administrative arena, an important support intended to help professionals in their work. In addition, the literature on supervision to which most have been exposed is primarily oriented to interactions with front-line workers (Kadushin, 1992; Shulman, 1992; Silberman, 1990).

This book extends the literature in professional supervision as it deals with issues of concern to managerial supervisors. Our intent is to familiarize these professionals with some of the major challenges that they encounter, to provide them with background information necessary to understand the issues, to illustrate the material with cases from the field, and to assist them in being more effective in their roles.

In addition to the gaps in the preparation of managerial supervisors, there are many tensions and pressures related to the world around us. Just as social problems are becoming increasingly more complex, the value orientations of our society are also changing dramatically. This creates a paradox for the professional when client and societal values clash.

Paradoxes have been identified as central themes in many of the chapters that follow. These paradoxes reflect the complexity of today's world in which competing choices and conflicting issues must be addressed. Paradoxes highlight the fact that there are no clear-cut solutions to today's complex problems. It is important for the managerial supervisor to exercise creativity and flexibility thoughtfully in handling these paradoxes.

In Part 1 of this volume, "The Changing Context," we discuss the broader environmental context of the human services as we enter the twenty-first century. Rapid social change and uncertain social, political, and economic environments create stressful and ambiguous situations faced by managerial supervisors within human service organizations.

Chapter 1, "Professional Challenges for Managerial Supervisors," provides an overview of the social and political environment in which human service organizations operate today. We identify the ideological, economic, social, and technological forces that shape our professional world and the professional challenges these present. We then focus on possible responses of the managerial supervisor and seek to stimulate independent thinking in meeting these challenges.

Critical legislation that impacts professionals within human service organizations is discussed in Chapter 2, "Responding to Legal Mandates." Information is provided about various laws that affect the workplace (e.g., The Family Leave Act, The Equal Opportunity Act, The Americans with Disabilities Act, and the Age Discrimination Act). Case examples are presented to familiarize managerial supervisors with the issues and approaches to be considered in meeting legal mandates.

The changing world of human services is creating new organizational realities as agencies must build strategic alliances with other human service organizations in order to survive. Many human service organizations are being affected, particularly smaller agencies. The work of professionals in these newly affiliated organizations requires attention, and this new and dramatic development is the subject of Chapter 3, "Building Strategic Alliances."

The past decade has brought with it the expectation that employees be technologically sophisticated and have computer access. The reality is, however, that managerial supervisors and front-line staff may be resistant to new technologies that are transforming the workplace. Staff training in this area is usually quite technical and requires workers to learn new skills. In Chapter 4, "Humanizing Technology," the approach is to engage the issues in relation to improving the quality of the services being offered and in decreasing the pressures on the worker.

Part 2, "Organizational Adaptive Strategies," targets some of the major professional challenges in the human services and focuses on hands-on approaches in dealing with them. Communication between managerial supervisors and employees is essential if organizations are to function in a healthy and productive manner. Chapter 5, "Facilitating Communication," focuses on the importance of the use of language, both verbal and written. In this chapter styles of communication, chain of command issues, the informal grapevine within organizations, and what information should be shared when and by whom are all addressed. Our assumption is that effective communication is the sine qua non for all organizational work.

Our focus on diversity appropriately follows the discussion of communication since cross-cultural communication is a critical element in improving intergroup relations both inside and outside the organization. Diversity is a complex subject since it includes such variables as ethnicity, religion, race, gender, age, disability, and sexual orientation. Chapter 6, "Supporting Diversity," examines the scope of diversity within both the staff and the client/consumer community and provides not only a practical way for managerial supervisors to work with the workers and their diverse clients, but also an overall approach to organizational development to address these issues.

Professionals are increasingly working in teams across disciplinary lines, the subject of Chapter 7, "Creating and Sustaining Interdisciplinary Teams." Staff members must have self-confidence in their professional identities, while also recognizing the importance of language as a common vehicle for understanding. Managerial supervisors must have the ability to help their staff members meet this challenge as the implications of being supervised by other disciplines create new expectations.

In Chapter 8, "Motivating, Appraising, and Rewarding," we discuss the complexity of establishing a reward-based culture while meeting the need for accountability through performance appraisals. A hands-on, how-to approach informs this discussion of a complex and essential administrative function required of managerial supervisors.

Managerial supervisors are confronted by agencies that are downsizing, by an increase in at-will dismissals, and by the loss of union protection. Chapter 9, "Protecting Managers as Workers," examines the personal costs faced by managerial supervisors. We seek to increase an understanding of, and provide a framework for, dealing with these stressors.

Effectiveness, and not just the efficiency of our programs, is the concern of our final chapter. Chapter 10, "Evaluating Program Effectiveness," examines meaningful approaches to program evaluation. The managerial supervisor plays a critical role in the evaluation of agency programs. In this discussion we highlight the need for both qualitative and quantitative data. The input of professional staff is central to the process.

The Epilogue provides a summation of the challenges faced by managerial supervisors, and we assess the forces that can contribute to both professional and personal satisfaction in a career well spent in the delivery of effective services to people in need.

Supervision is a critical element in the delivery of human services, intended to help professionals in their work with clients and consumer populations. This book extends the literature on supervision of the human services as it examines current critical issues of relevance to managerial supervisors. It uses case examples that have been developed by the authors, not actual organizational cases, to illustrate many of the concepts.

The intent is to provide new approaches to new problems and to provide new ideas to stimulate managerial supervisors to be innovative and proactive in their roles. There are no final answers to the complexities of professional work; the quest is to open options and empower people to be more confident and effective in their work. This book provides a starting point for addressing some of the major concerns and challenges of managerial supervisors, who supervise clinical supervisors and unit directors.

Acknowledgments

Human service professionals in leadership positions who are struggling with many of these issues stimulated our thinking and served to sharpen the focus of this book. Special acknowledgments are due to these leaders, many of whom are our former students, and to our current students, all of whom have challenged our thinking. They are too numerous to name here, but they are the ones who have caused us to recognize the importance of providing guidance for managerial supervisors.

This book also reflects the valuable input of many of our colleagues. We are particularly indebted to colleagues who read and contributed case materials to our chapters. These persons include Tom Armstrong, Russell Cardemone, Harold Goldman, Kelly NcNally Koney, Gary Johnson-McNutt, Eboney Kraisoraphong, Thomas Quick, and Jay Specter. Alma Martin and Juwanda Rowell provided administrative support in ways too numerous to mention. Diane Gilmore and Towanda Marner provided clerical assistance.

Special appreciation is due to those persons who encouraged and inspired us in writing this book: Frank Baskind, Nancy Lohmann, Roger Lohmann, Karl Netting, and Sharon Y. Robinson. Dan Perlmutter provided not only an array of conceptual challenges but also a sense of humor as he helped us cope with technology.

MANAGING HUMAN RESOURCES IN THE HUMAN SERVICES

PART ONE
THE CHANGING CONTEXT

IN this section, we discuss the broader environmental context of the human services. It is critically important that managerial supervisors understand how rapid social change and uncertain environments impact their work. Four chapters provide this overview.

Beginning with Chapter 1, "Professional Challenges for Managerial Supervisors," we examine how to maintain a professional identity in a turbulent professional human service environment. Chapter 2, "Responding to Legal Mandates," grounds our discussion through examples that illustrate the importance of various protections for employees in organizational practice. In Chapter 3, "Building Strategic Alliances," we guide the reader through the developmental stages and issues faced when managerial supervisors engage in building new interorganizational relationships. Last, we focus in Chapter 4, "Humanizing Technology," on how the workplace is being transformed through technological change.

It is our hope that the readers will use these chapters to assist them in analyzing the many issues and in handling the many challenges that they face in their professional work.

1

Professional Challenges for
Managerial Supervisors

Managing human resources in the human services has become increasingly complex and reflects the increasing complexity in our environment. The role of managerial supervisors is a critical one that requires a creative and adaptive approach to one's work.

Managerial supervisors are those professionals who are responsible for overseeing and evaluating the work performance and accountability of other persons within the human service agency. They may be located within various units and at all levels within these organizations. For example, managerial supervisors may be called unit managers, program coordinators, top level administrators, associate directors, or a host of other titles. What makes them managerial supervisors is that they have responsibility for supervising other employees. Their job requires that they be informed about a broad array of topics, such as new legislation and new technology, among others.

A managerial supervisor can be distinguised from a clinical supervisor in that the former is responsible for ensuring employee compliance with policies, regulations, procedures, rules, and protocols pertinent to agency operation. By contrast, the clinical supervisor oversees specific interventions with clients, focusing on the direct practice skills and techniques used by the worker.

The role of the managerial supervisor in the current environment can be compared to the leader of a jazz band, which extends the metaphor used by Slavin (1980) who described the human service administrator as the conductor of an orchestra. Both metaphors support Vaill's concept of leadership in his book entitled *Managing as a Performing Art: New Ideas for a World of Chaotic Change* (1991).

Yet the metaphor of the jazz band seems more appropriate today as it suggests the unexpected within a dynamic and volatile environment. dePree (1992) highlights the interdependence of the jazz band leader with the members of his group: "the effect of the performance depends on so many things—the environment, the volunteers in the band, the need for everybody to perform as individuals and as a group, the absolute dependence of the leader on the members of the band. . . . What a summary of an organization" (pp. 8–9). And this interdependence is very much a fundamental assumption of this book.

Our discussion of professional challenges for managerial supervisors throughout this volume focuses on the numerous paradoxes they will confront in their work.

WORKING WITH PARADOX

According to Webster's (1965, p. 610), a "paradox (as a person, condition, or act) is something with seemingly contradictory qualities or phases." Paradoxical situations therefore represent multiple simultaneous truths that managerial supervisors must be prepared to handle.

Fisher and Karger (1997) suggest the importance of examining the context in which paradoxes occur. They emphasize:

> knowing and understanding the connection between daily . . . practice and the structural dynamics of society—its history, political, and social and cultural dimensions. Contextualization assumes that individual, family, and community are also tied to larger structural

factors. At the heart . . . is an analysis of power and inequality and a social change ideology that translates this critical analysis into action. (p. 43)

It is our intent in this book to help managerial supervisors understand both the context and the content of their professional reality, as well as the importance of that understanding for action. Translating critical analysis into the daily actions of managerial supervisors takes perseverence and skill. In addition, it is not only useful but necessary to have a framework for dealing with professional paradoxes and to realize the dissonance they create for persons who work in human service organizations. This is especially important for those who seek traditional structures, clear rules, defined relationships, and any form of certainty. In today's world not only are the policies of human service organizations short lived due to the volatility of the social policy environment, but the career paths of professionals in these organizations, which once seemed somewhat linear, stable, and well defined, are no longer secure or predictable.

An understanding of the contextural paradoxes in which they operate helps managerial supervisors to work with change without unrealistic expectations that constrain their ability to practice. For managers at all levels, no longer is dichotomous thinking tolerated in the contemporary workplace; instead multilevel analysis is required. This chapter frames the total book as we present a series of significant professional issues, many of which are indeed paradoxical in nature and for which there are no clearcut or simple solutions. We hope that the mere identification of these issues will raise the reader's consciousness by bringing these issues to the fore and will also help managerial supervisors in human service organizations come to terms with a changing work reality that is increasingly turbulent (Emery & Trist, 1969).

TURBULENT ENVIRONMENTS

Ideological, economic, social, and technological forces are critical influences in the human service environment (Menefee, 1997; Perlmutter, 1987). Although these external elements have been highlighted in the literature over the years, radical shifts that are taking place in today's environment are creating conditions that have not been experienced previously (Jarman-Rhode, McFall, Kolar, & Strom, 1997), as illustrated further in this chapter.

> The more turbulent the times, the more complex the world, the more paradoxes there are. . . . Paradoxes are like the weather, something to be lived with, not solved, the worst aspects mitigated, the best enjoyed and used as clues to the way forward. Paradox has to be accepted, coped with, and made sense of, in life, in work, in the community, and among nations. (Handy, 1994, pp. 12–13)

Handy explicitly makes a link between changing conditions caused by these turbulent environments and paradoxes that serve to frame the challenges faced by managerial supervisors in their daily work.

IDEOLOGICAL FORCES

Politically there has been a dramatic reconfiguration in many Western societies as ideological orientations have shifted from a liberal, and even progressive orientation, to a conservative view of the world. Stern (1984) argues that the American value system has always been a conservative one and that the 50-year period from the New Deal to the Great Society was the exception, the result of an unusual coalition between government bureaucrats and special interest groups. "In bad times, government action could gain public and congressional support because something had to be done, but in better times, the appeals of self-reliance, the work ethic, and negative stereotypes of the poor made federal social-welfare actions less palatable" (Stern, 1984, p. 5). Consequently "getting government off our backs" has become the prevailing ethos as Americans are increasingly self-oriented and as a communitarian philosophy of social responsibility is increasingly abandoned. Etzioni (1993) has called for a communitarian philosophy of social responsibility and civic entrepreneurship to counter the isolationist trends of our times. For example, (Henton, Melville, & Walesh, 1997) write:

> Born of fundamental economic, political, technological and demographic shifts, a new kind of leader is emerging to help Amer-

ica's communities as they enter an era of continuous change. . . .
Civic entrepreneurs help communities collaborate to develop and
organize their economic assets and to build strong, resilient networks between and among the public, private and civil sectors.

The collaboration between the for-profit and the nonprofit sectors as well as the merger of agencies are trends that must be
taken seriously, especially as the public sector sheds its responsibility for the provision of services. The consequences of these
changes are important as there are fewer arenas for civic participation at both board and program levels. Lohmann (1992) views
this as resulting in the erosion of "The Commons," which he defines as the arena of citizen involvement in communal activity, so
vital to a democracy.

How these new relationships will develop remains to be seen.
Not only are nonprofit human service organizations competing
increasingly among themselves (McMurtry, Netting, & Kettner,
1990) but also with the corporate sector (Perlmutter, 1997). Ideological shifts pave the way for the new movement toward privatization (Perlmutter & Adams, 1990), a development yet to be
proven effective.

Professional politics are part of the social context as well. In
this climate of reduced sensitivity to the plight of disadvantaged
groups, there are changes in the orientations and behaviors expected of managerial staff. For example, managers who have been
trained in the clinical professions must reorient their thinking to
acquire a more business-like mentality. Years of professional training and experience are no longer valued as the emphasis has
shifted to the bottom line. One must be fiscally sophisticated and
accountability oriented. In some agencies the unit directors receive bonuses if they obtain grants, correct error rates, and generate business for the agency. This is a far cry from past professional expectations in the human services, in which managers
focused on enhancing relationships. The politics of the workplace
becomes quite different in a climate in which the values have so
dramatically shifted.

Empowerment, a long espoused value of the social work profession (Shera & Page, 1995), has not only captured the attention
of other service-oriented professionals, but of the business com-

munity as well. Peters (1992) and Thomas and Velthouse (1990), among others, address empowerment in the management literature and Bass (1990) links it to "transformational leadership." The dilemma for managerial supervisors is one of balancing the importance of nurturing their staffs to feel empowered while responding to their agency's pressures for efficiency and accountability.

The advocacy role of human service professionals is a critical one as they are in a special position to see unmet needs. And yet, maintaining the advocacy role within human service organizations, never simple to achieve (Ostrander, 1989), becomes all the more paradoxical in the current context. Nonprofits, often dependent on external grants and contracts, are in a compromised position if they become advocates and thus "bite the hand that feeds them."

As a result, the argument has been made that agencies that provide services to clients cannot be effective advocates because of their dependency on external funding sources (Goldman, 1997). Instead, the advocacy function must be lodged in advocacy organizations or professional associations that can freely identify problems and bring issues to the public. This is in contrast to the strong view taken by Gibelman and Kraft (1996), who argue that advocacy must be part of the ongoing leadership role in all human service organizations, a long held and clearly articulated position by the profession of social work (Richan, 1980; Kramer, 1981). Unfortunately the many pressures for survival faced by human service organizations often puts advocacy at the bottom of the list of roles played by their executives (Perlmutter & Adams, 1994). Both arguments merit examination to ensure the fulfillment of the advocacy role by human service organizations.

A final point related to ideological forces is the fact that as human service systems are changing, traditional professional roles are being challenged. New collaborations are creating new conditions and new problems (Netting & Williams, 1996). How do health professionals, MBAs, social workers, public administrators, and other professionals bridge their different value frameworks, techniques, and service approaches as they work with individual clients in these new complex organizations? This is directly related to the use of teams, which is clearly the wave of the future (Gummer, 1995), and which affects how leaders lead (Steckler & Fondas, 1995), how performance measurement systems are designed, and how problems are solved (Pacanowsky, 1995). The paradox for leadership is that a new set of values is needed to underpin the new roles and skills that are required (Drucker, 1992).

ECONOMIC FORCES

The economic dimension calls attention to the impact of a global economy on human service organizations in several ways. Menefee (1997) highlights the pros and cons of this development. A pro is the opportunity for human service organizations to expand into other societies, as is already the case of United Way and CARE; a con is the economic reality that they must compete simultaneously for scarce resources.

Fisher and Karger (1977) note the paradox that although the world is becoming smaller as globalization is increasing, the human service world is getting more isolated and alienated. Jobs are being lost and more low-skilled workers are being displaced. Multinational corporations have broader interests and locally based corporations have lost their identification with, their commitment to, and their responsibility for the economic and social well-being of their home-based communities (Reich, 1992).

Other economic aspects must be noted. Since the nonprofit sector has been plagued by some sad examples of fiscal wrongdoing, as illustrated by United Way of America and New Era Philanthropy, managerial supervisors must wrestle with the paradox of maintaining professional credibility and integrity in a context of public skepticism and distrust of the organizations in which they work (Gibelman, Gelman, & Pollack, 1997; Young, Bania, & Bailey, 1996).

New organizational structures are emerging as financing mechanisms for human services are changing. For example, managed care approaches create an entirely different set of assumptions, understandings, and incentives. Seasoned professionals who were educated in fee-for-service systems are now dealing with capitated systems. Not only does this mean retooling to understand the economics of managed care systems, but it means understanding that what was viewed as a responsible economic arrangement is no longer a reasonable economic response. For example, health care providers could earn more money by seeing consumers in fee-for-service systems in which every time the consumer was served, a payment was attached. Now, with managed care, a capitated approach means that consumers who are heavy users of services will have to be balanced by those who are not heavy users if the agency is to survive. The entire way of thinking about what "makes sense" economically has to shift as risk increases for those agencies that target clients with the greatest needs. Incentives are in place to serve whose who demand, or require, less.

As doors are being opened to private sector players to compete for and participate in the delivery of human services, the economic impact will be great. Since nonprofits do not have access to capital, they cannot sell stock or borrow money; their usual solution is to get bigger in order to survive. Furthermore, there is little to assure us that the consumer's interests, as opposed to the stockholder's interests, will be primary, a problem that has sharply surfaced in the health care arena. Thus, Dezendorf (1997) warns that it is necessary to be very cautious in moving to privatization since "the definition of privatization, the characteristics of the privatization process, and even the outcomes are being debated. Little solid and generally accepted research exists" (p. 1). Since this is the direction toward which this nation is taking a headlong plunge, it is incumbent on human service management, at all levels, to monitor the process carefully and to ensure that effectiveness of the services being delivered does not get lost in the process.

SOCIAL FORCES

The above discussion of ideological and economic forces leads directly to a discussion of the social context. Racial divisions and balkanization are increasing, as is the gap between the rich and the poor. At the same time, public concern with the needs of poor, sick, elderly, and disabled persons is decreasing. In spite of the many human needs that must be met, the support for education, welfare, employment, and training has sharply eroded. This is reflected in the welfare reform legislation of 1996.

The common goal of service to clients or society no longer

serves as the glue for cohesion between administration and staff. Rather, increased problems in society lead to much more stressful work conditions, while at the same time lack of funds to support human services creates poorer working conditions, both in terms of salaries and benefits for professionals. This in turn leads, all too often, to ongoing conflict in the human services as the views of management and professionals diverge.

TECHNOLOGICAL FORCES

Technological advances are certainly an important part of the human service environment. However, the challenges created by technology are not new. The complexity of developing effective and efficient management information systems, a problem since the 1970s (Holland, 1976; Weirich, 1980), is still not resolved. A continuing technological challenge is how to make the best use of agency data for accountability purposes. And although the extensive use of voicemail may be economical, it is not clear what the effect is on clients/consumers who are under duress, who need to contact their professional caregivers, but who cannot follow the complicated directions required to obtain human contact. This example touches on only some of the elements of technology but serves to set the stage for our later discussion on humanizing technology.

PROFESSIONAL CHALLENGES

The forces just discussed contribute to the turbulent environment within which human service managerial supervisors perform their roles. We now explore the professional challenges faced by managerial supervisors as they deal with this array of demanding circumstances, often unique to the human services, as well as their professional identity and performance.

We have identified three challenges as particularly relevant to this discussion of professionalism: (1) the blurring of the boundaries between the for-profit, nonprofit, and public sectors, (2) the impact of changing public policy on human service organizations, and (3) the requirements associated with the increasing use of teams and new forms of professional collaborations.

The first challenge—the blurring of the boundaries in the human services between the profit, nonprofit, and public sectors—is a phenomenon that became prominent in the early 1990s but that has been sharply accelerated by the end of the decade. Thus the emergence of for-profits in the human services, an area traditionally reserved for the nonprofit and public sectors, has had a dramatic impact on the field. New approaches and new technologies, not always viewed as client oriented, have changed the nature of professional activity. Furthermore, the high salaries offered by for-profits have created a drain as highly trained professionals have opted to increase their earning potential. Although this phenomenon is most obvious in the field of day care and child care, it is affecting the criminal justice system as prisons are being privatized, among other services.

The second challenge—the impact of public policy on the human services—is being felt throughout the country. Most dramatic are the changes in health and mental health services as managed care has taken hold. Consequently policies and decisions are being made not by the dominant profession in that domain but by business interests and the stockholders, and are not based on client/patient interests and needs. Managerial supervisors are often the bearer of the bad tidings when services are cut, standards are changed, and jobs are lost to reductions in the workforce. This is a far cry from the professional dominance and autonomy that have traditionally characterized a profession.

Managerial supervisors are certainly affected by the impact of these two challenges. Not only must they supervise people who have now entered the field with fewer qualifications, as deprofessionalization in the human services increases, but they must also deal with the pressures for efficiency and cost saving, as opposed to effectiveness and meeting consumer needs.

The third challenge concerning teams and collaborations focuses on the professional issues faced by supervisors and managers in a delivery system in which the knowledge, skills, and values of multiple professionals are required, and which inevitably often compete with one another. New collaborations create new conditions and new opportunities. How do mental health and health professionals, MBAs, social workers, and other involved professionals bridge their different value frameworks, techniques, and service approaches as they work with individual clients in an array of new and complex organizations? A sine-qua-non in this discussion of professional challenges is the fundamental prerequisite of individual flexibility and adaptability as new behaviors are required to meet new, often unpredictable circumstances.

Health and human service managerial supervisors know that persons from different professions bring different socializations to their work, and they must also know how to maximize these multiple strengths for the good of the collective. Supervisors often experience the somewhat paradoxical nature of their roles as they work with staff persons who want to feel valued as individuals and unique as professionals in fast-paced and uncertain workplace climates. They must deal with anger over the downgrading of positions that were believed to be "owned" by particular professional groups, yet they must be open to considering new staffing patterns. For example, positions once requiring a masters degree are now held by nonprofessional bachelor degree graduates.

Managerial supervisors must be sensitive to what employees face as a new generation of professionals enters the workplace armed with recently acquired knowledge, values, and skills, only to find that they are not the only professionals performing the roles specified in their job descriptions. For example, in many health care settings social workers, nurses, rehabilitation counselors, and a range of other professionals may all be hired as case managers (Netting & Williams, 1996). Supervisees will consequently draw their knowledge base from multiple disciplines in the work setting while at the same time, in the interest of survival, may want to institutionalize their own profession within the contemporary human service delivery system. Balancing professional identities with interdisciplinary practice is essential in the contemporary workplace, and the managerial supervisor must be a leader in making this happen.

When they supervise persons from a variety of professions, managerial supervisors also know that each profession has its own standards and codes of ethics, and one profession cannot be held accountable to the code of another. Supervisors, then, must be familiar with various professional standards and become "multicultural" in how they approach their role. For example, if a human service manager supervises social workers, nurses, and physical therapists, the supervisor must know what is expected in each professional category and in each separate code of ethics, while simultaneously encouraging the development of a common language so that interprofessional relationships can develop. In addition, the managerial supervisor must be aware of boundaries established in state credentialing laws so that only persons with appropriate licenses perform those tasks designated by law. Keeping up with change on these various levels is not easy, but is essential to effective contemporary human service management.

WHAT CAN A MANAGERIAL
SUPERVISOR DO?

Based on the professional challenges just discussed, we believe that there are ways that managerial supervisors can be more effective. First, it is essential to create an *organizational culture* that both unites diverse professionals and supports and recognizes their unique expertise. Second, managerial supervisors must develop (1) an in-depth awareness of their own *professional identity* and a recognition of what other professionals bring to the organization, (2) an up-to-date knowledge base about multiple professional requirements and standards, and (3) the leadership ability to mobilize this awareness and knowledge into action.

One way for managerial supervisors to make sense of this struggle for professional identity is to view professions as cultures. This means recognizing that people are socialized to their profession, its values and artifacts, and seeking to understand how they will work with others. An understanding of the powerful nature of these professional subcultures is useful in dealing with the many tensions that surface among supervisees.

Clark (1997) states that the education and training of professionals "shape their identities, values, and norms of practice in certain ways that may either enhance or inhibit effective communication and collaboration" (p. 441). Clark contends that to provide quality of care, there must be ways of preserving individual professional identities while simultaneously "creating a common ground where differences are valued because of their unique contribution" (p. 441). This supervisory task poses quite a challenge, especially since the development of a common organizational culture is essential, viewed "as the social or normative glue that holds an organization together" (Jones & May, 1992, p. 258).

Cultures are deep and complex, and are often difficult to understand. Schein (1992) defines culture as:

> A pattern of basic assumptions—invented, discovered, or developed by a given group as it learns to cope with its problems of external adaptation and internal integration—that has worked well enough to be considered valid and therefore, to be taught to new members as the correct way to perceive, think, and feel in relation to those problems. (p. 9)

He sees culture as having three levels: (1) artifacts that are the visible elements of a culture, (2) values that are stated or espoused by the culture, and (3) underlying assumptions that are not always so evident.

Professional artifacts come in various forms. They not only can be the products of a profession (i.e., clients served and reports produced) but they can also be the concrete symbols that the larger society recognizes (i.e., the language or jargon of the group).

Professional cultures have values. These espoused values are those that are publicly recognized and are typically contained in codes of ethics. For example, in 1996 the National Association of Social Workers (NASW) approved a revised Code of Ethics detailing the standards and basic principles that guide the profession. Supervisory managers who are social workers by training will use this code to guide their expectations of and behavior toward their supervisees.

Last, professional cultures have basic underlying assumptions that, according to Thomas (1991), are held onto tenaciously. These underlying assumptions are usually instilled during a person's educational process as part of their professional socialization process and may be so taken for granted that professionals perform their roles without consciously recognizing how these assumptions drive their practice. Supervisory managers will encounter conflict and misunderstanding within their units or organizations when the underlying assumptions of different professional cultures clash. For example, the social work culture is grounded in the concept of client self-determination, an assumption that delimits the role of the professional; this concept may not be embraced as strongly by cultures of other helping professions.

Resistance to change is heavily rooted in professional assumptions. Schein (1992) explains that cultural assumptions serve as lenses or filters for understanding the environment. Without these filters, there is a tendency to feel somewhat overwhelmed and uncertain, even anxious. Because each of us has assumptions that guide what is done, to give up long held assumptions is anxiety producing. In the current world of human services, where change is the norm, it is not surprising that even those professionals who define themselves as change agents often cling tenaciously to the assumptions that have stabilized their worlds. Group identification with a profession is grounded in these roots or basic assumptions, which form the core of professional identity.

FACING SUPERVISORY CHALLENGES

There are several approaches to these challenges that require thoughtful analysis, information gathering, and planning.

AWARENESS OF SELF AND OTHERS

To fully appreciate the roots of diverse professional cultures, supervisors must first recognize the relevance of their own professional identity. It is as critically important for supervisors and managers to be self-aware, as it is for persons who perform direct practice or clinical roles. Supervisors must be aware of the history that drives their professional socialization because it is within that history that the grand narratives and great traditions of their professions have emerged (Kreuger, 1997). In a time when the managers of health and human service organizations may have backgrounds in business, public administration, health administration, and social work, managerial supervisors will be critically aware that their educational experiences have been different. Coming to terms with the implications of these differences, and realizing that there are strengths that each profession brings to the whole, is essential for the managerial supervisor's comfort level. Learning to communicate in a language that can be shared by professional administrators and managers who are from different fields is also necessary for the managerial supervisor in order to successfully represent and convey staff concerns to agency leaders.

In addition, supervisors will not always supervise persons from the same profession as their own. It is very likely that they will supervise persons from multiple disciplines, paraprofessionals, and even volunteers. If supervisors are aware of their own professional biases and feel confident in their professional identities, they will likely be more effective in dealing with the conflicts that arise when values inevitably clash. If supervisors know what underlying assumptions they bring to their work, the visceral responses felt when a supervisee does something that is considered inappropriate may be better contained and understood.

For example, a social work supervisor in a health care organization felt herself reacting harshly when she heard a nurse tell a family member that "your mother is 85 and has broken her hip. In this situation you may want to think about assisted living for her." This suggestion was made before the nurse had seen the mother and was based on her experience with other older persons who had broken hips. The supervisor's visceral reaction was based on an underlying assumption of self-determination and autonomy grounded in the social work code of ethics. The nurse was erring on the side of beneficence and safety, wanting very much to protect this older woman. The supervisor realized that she had reacted strongly because of the conflict in values between self-determination and beneficence. On the other hand, as a supervisor she tried to affirm the care expressed by her supervisee in wanting to protect an older client, while pointing out the need for her to talk with the older woman to see what her wishes might be and to consider the option that she might be able to return home.

It is also important for the supervisor to understand that professional cultures are only one of the many cultural dynamics within organizations. Entire units (of same or different professionals) will develop their own subcultures within organizations just as workers will bring their own personal cultural backgrounds to the workplace. Insight into the complex nature of the workplace is, on many levels, a multicultural experience.

MAINTAINING UP-TO-DATE KNOWLEDGE

Awareness is critical, but maintaining up-to-date knowledge is also necessary for effective supervision. There are multiple types of knowledge that supervisors must continually update.

First, supervisors are challenged to keep up to date on substantive information that is relevant to the type of work that is done in their organization. For example, a supervisor in child protective services must understand the field of child welfare, know the latest research that informs practice, and be cognizant of the multiple changes in federal and state policies that guide agency operations. Not only is the supervisor's knowledge base continually being updated, but the supervisor must be certain that supervisees also have opportunities to upgrade their knowledge and skills. Continuing education and in-service and on-the-job training are not only beneficial to the individuals who participate in these events but keep the core service delivery competencies of the organization relevant.

Second, supervisors must constantly upgrade their knowledge of the managerial field, one in which popular books are being published in rapid succession. What are the latest advances in management practice and how might they be applied to the supervisor's situation? In this book we are trying to provide that very thing—an update on what managerial and supervisory knowledge will guide managerial supervisors in our rapidly changing environment.

Third, it is necessary for supervisors to have updated information on the requirements of and changes in various licensure laws, standards, and guidelines so that employees are appropriately credentialed and guided in their work.

For example, one supervisor found himself in a situation in which he was responsible for supervising workers who entered three different jurisdictions in the course of their daily practice—the Commonwealth of Virginia, the State of Maryland, and the District of Columbia. All three varied in their licensure requirements for clinical practice. Because services were being delivered to clients located in three different jurisdictions by these same workers, the supervisor needed to be knowledgeable about whom he hired and where they were licensed. Potential employees from each of the three states asked him how the licensure laws differed and what they would have to do to sit for the various required examinations, and he had to be able to explain the requirements and to advise accordingly.

Professionals will have to meet different requirements to maintain their credentials. For example, nurses have to have a certain number of documented continuing education units to maintain their licenses; similarly, chaplains who are members of The Association of Professional Chaplains will need to document their continuing education units. Depending on the profession, these requirements will differ. Supervisors must seek ways to support employees in getting to conferences and attending events that are necessary for them to upgrade their knowledge and skills, and that are necessary for their continuing credentialing.

PROVIDING EFFECTIVE LEADERSHIP

Both awareness and knowledge are critical to effective leadership, but the work does not stop there. The supervisor must mobilize awareness and knowledge into effective action (Bailey & Koney, 1996). Schein (1992) provides some clues regarding organizational cultures that can be helpful to managerial supervisors. These include, for example, those incidents the leaders consider critical and that are measured and controlled, the deliberate role modeling and teaching by leaders, and the criteria for the allocation of rewards and status including promotions. Schein also calls attention to the design of physical space, as well as the stories, legends, and myths about important organizational happenings.

If supervisors want to embed within the organization a cultural assumption about collaboration being important, they need to reinforce this assumption at every opportunity, they must be very intentional in defining their expectations, and they must be sensitive to how these expectations are received by their staff. If leaders are inconsistent in what they focus on, chances are that the opportunity to instill a culture of collaboration will not be realized.

For example, a supervisor in a hospice program wanted to emphasize the importance of teaming among nurses, social workers, physicians, and chaplains. She arranged team meetings in which they could all meet together on a regular basis, adopted a multidimensional assessment tool that was to be completed by a team rather than by an individual, encouraged colleagues to make joint visits to their clients, and conducted in-services on the importance of teaming. Her consistent actions over time contributed to the developing value of interdisciplinary teaming. Eventually, new persons entering her employ were struck by the fact that they were as likely to be visiting their clients with team members as alone and that in team meetings everyone's voice was heard. Teaming was an assumed cultural value.

When crises occur, supervisors are under pressure to act. Because crises are a time of high anxiety, staff look to managers and supervisors for direction and what is done will be remembered. These times are also opportunities in which "legends" develop. A supervisor in a large multiservice agency found himself in a crisis situation when he had to reduce the budget for his unit. Having promoted the concept of services being more important than administrative costs, staff wondered if this espoused value would really hold when "push came to shove." The supervisor's decision to cut administrative costs and not to touch the salaries of staff was viewed as consistent with the established culture and was remembered as a "gutsy move in which he did the right thing." Years later staff would refer to the supervisor who cared about them and relate the somewhat embellished story of this event. We believe that leaders in health and human service organizations are continually developing and molding, and setting the tone, for the units in which they work if not for the entire organization. This is essentially how organizational cultures develop. Leaders literally embed culture.

Contemporary managerial supervisors are often trying to embed a culture that addresses a basic paradox—that of balancing a healthy respect for professional identities, roles, and relationships with the need to instill a cultural value of collaboration and teaming across multiple professional groups. This means that supervisees continue to have their own professional roots and assumptions, but that there are common unit or organizational roots that also must be embraced. As long as these assumptions can coexist, then leaders stand a chance of literally getting them to "root."

IMPLICATIONS FOR MANAGERIAL SUPERVISORS

The ultimate consequence of these various facets of our turbulent professional environment is the introduction of a field of uncertainty.

> Uncertainty—in the economy, society, politics—has become so great as to render futile, if not counter-productive, the kind of planning most companies still practice: forecasting based on probabilities. . . .
>
> Every . . . commitment is based on assumptions about the future. To arrive at them, traditional planning asks, "What is most likely to happen?" Planning for uncertainty asks, instead, "What has already happened that will create the future . . . ?"
>
> Successful innovations exploit changes that have already happened. . . . They exploit the time lag . . . between the change itself and its perception and acceptance. (Drucker, 1995, pp. 39–40)

Drucker's response to the issue of uncertainty is to highlight the importance of proactive leadership that can adapt to the changes that have taken place by concentrating on the organization's special strengths.

A paradox is evident here, as Drucker (1995) points out. Although proactive leadership is critical in the nonprofit world, the enormous demands in the system just to keep afloat serve to inhibit proactive behavior. At the same time, the issue of strategic decision making as an important aspect of leadership is receiving increasing attention (Gummer, 1997). "The key role that intellectual ability plays in strategic decision making highlights the fact in the post-industrial era, the success of a corporation lies more in its intellectual and systems capabilities than in its physical assets" (p. 87).

An example of proactive leadership and strategic decision making in a very complex system can be found in a major metropolitan Health Department in which the Commissioner of Health took the initiative in designing a unique response to the newly developing managed care environment. The state was issuing a request for proposal for the provision of mental health services oriented to the nonprofit and for-profit sectors. The Commissioner was the only commissioner in the state to develop a response in which the public County Department of Mental Health and Mental Retardation would be the provider of services. Her proposal was accepted and the program was funded under public auspice. The use of systems understanding, creativity, and the political process illustrate effective and proactive leadership.

A second example of effective leadership concerns the paradox of seeking new organizational leaders both on the board of directors and in the management cohort who can deal with the technical aspects of finance, public relations, and legal issues. Yet, at the same time, the urgency exists to educate, inform, and sometimes inculcate these new actors with the ideology that originally served as the impetus for the agency's existence and for the underpinnings of its mission statement.

Women's Scope, a fund-raising body for an array of women's services, was faced with this dilemma as original board members, who were committed to the organizational cultural assumptions about social change and social action, retired. Yet, incoming members were faced with the very dramatic reality of supporting the survival of member agencies; raising money became their key priority. How not to lose sight of the mission of the system and its unique culture while struggling for survival was a serious challenge, and much thought was being given to board orientation and education.

This challenge was of primary concern to the managerial staff of this social change fund: the elder trustees were the keepers of the flame, embued with institutional memory concerning the original mission of the organization, in contrast to the new cohort, which was recruited for specific expertise in areas such as taxes or legal matters, investment know-how, or public relations. Question arose concerning how to combine the two orientations, that of the broader commitment to mission and that of special technical expertise. Managerial supervisors were an active part of the planning process as induction sessions and retreats were designed to address these concerns.

CONCLUSION

How can professionals in the human services who are being affected by these changes be helped in this time of radical change (Boyett & Henry, 1991)? Professionals are often anxious and uneasy as they experience multiple paradoxes in their work environment. The challenge is not only to make the work environment conducive not only to the effective provision of service to its consumers, but also to create an environment conducive to a good feeling among the professional staff members about their competency and about their role in society. A first step in managing paradoxes and devising solutions is understanding the multiple issues.

As we gave thought to this book, it was clear that inadequate attention has been paid to managerial supervisors or to the contemporary issues that affect their professional performance (Perlmutter, 1983). In this first chapter we have identified an array of pressures and paradoxes that are being experienced in human service organizations. In the chapters that follow we explore professional issues that are directly related to the subject of that chapter. In suggesting approaches for managerial supervisors in the agency setting, our intent is not to provide ready solutions, but rather to stimulate an array of responses on the part of the supervisor that is syntonic with their supervisees' needs, the organization's goals, and their own professional style.

2

Responding to Legal Mandates

Coauthored With Karen Cherwony

One of the greatest indicators of a turbulent environment is the rapid change taking place in human resource practices, policies, and laws. The managerial supervisor must be aware of the continuous state of flux in which our society resides as a result of new case law and administrative implementation. It is therefore essential that managerial supervisors be aware that this is a changing field, that laws are continuously being developed and passed, and that it is essential to remain updated in the legal arena.

In this chapter we identify some of the major legal issues that managerial supervisors will encounter. Our discussion is framed around specific cases that place the material in the human service arena and demonstrate the complexity and interrelationships of various legal mandates. It is not our intention to provide legal advice, which should be obtained from appropriate legal sources.

WHY ARE LEGAL ISSUES PARADOXICAL?

Several paradoxes arise from the legal context that affects organizational, professional, and personal dimensions in human service agency work. *On an organizational level one paradox is that just as nonprofit providers of human services have been highly valued in this country, today their autonomy and the authority of their governing boards of directors are clearly being challenged and questioned.* For example, much of the responsibility for agency decision making and policy making is shifting from the agencies themselves to a situation in which these agencies must adhere to public policy. Although in the past nonprofits certainly had to adhere to broad public policy mandates as they sought state legal sanction, their boards were able to make many governance decisions and feel reasonably in control of internal agency operations. The laws to be discussed in this chapter place sharp constraints and limits on agency and board decision making in private nonprofit and for-profit agencies that deliver human services.

On a professional level a second paradox exists. *Just as agency autonomy is being challenged, so too is the nature of professional practice being challenged, and even violated, by the new legal mandates.* For example, although professional practice assumes confidentiality regarding client disclosures, the employing organization's need for information can impinge on the professional standard of privacy. A paradox is created for the professional who seeks to protect the client and is concerned about possible access to and use of agency data.

On a personal level a third paradox exists. *Just as supervisors and managers are educated to perform their duties in a professional manner, these same professionals often feel overwhelmed and may even feel betrayed when confronted with a legal challenge.* We contend that personal reactions will always enter the situation, regardless of how clear the professional and/or organizational issue is.

For example, Dr. Childers was sued for malpractice when his patient, Mr. Martin, died on a basketball court. Dr. Childers had clearly explained to Mr. Martin that his cardiac condition was unstable and he could not resume his athletic activities at this time. Mr. Martin, an avid neighborhood basketball player, played against the physician's advice, and died on the court. The jury was clearly sympathetic to the widow and her three children, and in the course of the trial Dr. Childers felt victimized as he was accused of poor medical care and irresponsible professional behavior. Of significance for our discussion is the fact that he was not offered support from his employing organization or from his colleagues. As a result, he felt embittered, betrayed, and alienated from his place of work even though he was providing high quality professional care and was a highly regarded physician in a prestigious institution.

Thus it is essential that managerial supervisors know what to do and what not to do from an organizational perspective, from a professional perspective, and from a personal perspective. Supervision must be multifaceted, dealing with the administrative, educational, and supportive elements elucidated by Kadushin (1992), and the managerial supervisor must constantly recognize the implications of various legal mandates that influence agency practice.

WHAT MUST WE KNOW AND WHEN MUST WE KNOW IT?

Different legal elements are relevant to various situations that arise in the workplace. We have selected several cases that illustrate the complexities involved and will discuss the particular legal aspects pertinent to these cases. Keep in mind that this is just an introduction to some of the legal mandates that can influence one's work.

THE LEGAL CONTEXT OF THE HIRING PROCESS

There are many steps in the hiring process that are regulated by federal laws and regulations as well as state fair-employment practices statutes (Sheets & Bushardt, 1994). These include recruitment, the use of application forms, reference checks, interviews, medical examinations, and tests. To illustrate the nature of hiring regulations, we use Anita Simpson as an example.

Anita Simpson, a professional who wears a hearing aid, is applying for a position as recreation therapist in a large nonprofit residential program for recovering alcohol and drug-dependent delinquent youth. The agency is located in a suburban area of the city, with poor public transportation. In addition, recent staff layoffs require flexibility on the part of all the agency's professionals to do general coverage once a month on weekends and once a week in the evenings. During the course of the hiring process Ms. Simpson is interviewed by the director of the recreational therapy program, by the director of the overall agency, and by the night supervisor. The job and the flexibility required are described in detail by the director of recreational therapy who focuses on Ms. Simpson's experience and qualifications for the job. The executive director focuses on the cultural background of most of the clients, and wonders how Ms. Simpson's own personal life experience will affect her performance in this setting. He also questions if her hearing impairment could affect her work with the negative and hostile teenagers she will encounter in this setting. The night supervisor focuses on the realities of the work shift at night, including the problem of transportation. In the process he asks whether Ms. Simpson has children, which could create a problem for her evening work, and if she and her husband have only one car, would the car be available for her use?

There are several federal laws that directly impact the hiring process, as illustrated by Ms. Simpson's situation. Title VII of the Civil Rights Act of 1964 prohibits employment discrimination on the basis of race, national origin, sex, or religion. The employer cannot use the interview or the application process to obtain any information that might have a "disparate impact." A selection procedure is discriminatory if it disproportionately screens out members of a protected group and is neither job related nor justified by business necessity. Interviewers should be familiar with the Equal Employment Opportunity Commission's (EEOC) Uniform Guidelines on Employee Selection Procedures published in the Federal Register, p. 38290, on August 25, 1978. As a general rule, all questions eliciting protected class information (e.g., race, color, sex, age, disability) should be eliminated from applications and interviews unless kept on a separate form for affirmative action or EEO reporting and recordkeeping purposes, or a protected characteristic is a bona fide occupational qualification for the position being filled.

The EEOC and the courts have recognized that questions about marital status, pregnancy, child bearing, child care, or the number and ages of an applicant's children may constitute unlawful gender-based discrimination if used to deny or limit employment opportunities. If this type of information is needed for tax, insurance, or social security purposes, it should be obtained after employment and recorded on a separate form, not on the application or during an interview.

Discrimination against applicants or employees because of non-job-related mental and/or physical handicaps or disabilities is prohibited by federal laws and regulations as well as numerous state and local laws. The Americans With Disabilities Act (ADA) of 1990 prohibits a covered employer from asking applicants about the existence of, and nature or severity of his or her disability at the preoffer stage (Burgdorf, 1991; Dart, 1993). Inquiries about the applicant's ability to perform the essential functions of a job with or without reasonable accommodation are permitted, however. These questions should not be phrased in terms of disability. In Ms. Simpson's case, she should not have been asked if her hearing impairment would impact her work with teenagers. She may be asked what experience she has had communicating with hostile teenagers. Information on prohibited and permitted inquiries under the ADA are published by the EEOC.

In 1997 the EEOC passed new guidelines to carry out the ADA, which "told employers that they may not discriminate against qualified workers with mental illness, may not ask job applicants if they have a history of mental illness and must take reasonable steps to accommodate employees with psychiatric or emotional problems" (*New York Times*, April 30, 1997, pp. A1, D22).

Other federal laws relevant to the hiring phase include the following:

- The Equal Pay Act, which requires equal pay for equal work;
- The Age Discrimination in Employment Act of 1967, as amended, which protects individuals between the ages of 40 and 70;
- The Rehabilitation Act of 1973, which protects handicapped employees;
- The Pregnancy Discrimination Act of 1978, which protects pregnant applicants and employees; and

- The Immigration Reform and Control Act (IRCA) of 1986, which prohibits employers from hiring or continuing to employ illegal immigrants who are not authorized to work in the United Sates and establishes an elaborate verification process. To comply with IRCA, the employer must ask applicants whether they are authorized to work in the United States, require them to present the authorization documentation required, but otherwise avoid asking applicants about their national origin or place of birth.

Furthermore, agencies with federal contracts must be informed about other legislation (e.g., The Vietnam Readjustment Act of 1974). It is essential that management clarify which laws apply to their particular agency and inform all supervisory managers of these laws. In addition to the federal laws listed above, it is necessary to be familiar with the regulations adopted by the federal agencies that have the responsibility for implementing the laws.

Individual states and local governments may also have laws, regulations, and guidelines that can be stricter than the federal ones or can cover areas not covered at the federal level. One example is local policy that bans employment discrimination based on sexual orientation.

Temple University's statement provides an example of an organization's response to the legal environment at the federal, state, and local levels:

TEMPLE UNIVERSITY IS COMMITTED TO A POLICY OF EQUAL OPPORTUNITY for all in every aspect of its operations. The University has pledged not to discriminate on the basis of race, color, sex, age, religion, national origin, sexual orientation, marital status, or disability. . . . Affirmative action at Temple has these inclusive objectives: . . . To employ and advance in employment qualified women, minorities, individuals with disabilities, disabled veterans and veterans of the Vietnam era. (Graduate Bulletin, 1996–1998, Inside Cover)

The statement informs employees whom to contact for more information about their rights.

Many of the questions asked in the interview process with Ms.

Simpson were illegal in that they violated both Title VII of the Civil Rights Act of 1964 and The Americans With Disabilities Act of 1990. It was a violation to ask about her husband, her car, her children, and her hearing ability. The only subject that could have appropriately been discussed in the hiring interview were Ms. Simpson's professional background, the requirements of the job, and whether she felt that she could meet them. If she had not been hired by the agency on the basis of the illegal questions that were asked, the agency could have been sued. To avoid these problems, limit all preemployment inquiries, oral or written, on applications or in interviews, to questions necessary to assess the candidate's ability and suitability to perform the functions of the job. To limit the subjectivity inherent in any interviewing process and vulnerability to charges of discrimination, management should provide specific help to supervisors. For example, agencies could

- devise questions that are as objective as possible and clearly job related;
- provide guidelines and training for interviewers;
- use multiple interviewers;
- ask the same questions the same way to all candidates; and
- continually monitor the hiring process for discriminatory effects.

THE LEGAL CONTEXT OF PERSONAL LEAVE

Once hired, a number of legal issues can arise about the employment status of the individual. Next, we present a complex situation that must be carefully evaluated since several laws are involved. Concerns in this case focus on a personal leave situation.

Jerome Jessup is an outstanding employee who has worked as a van driver for an agency serving older adults for 15 years. He is always sensitive to the needs of older persons and is counted on by his supervisor. The agency has its central office in Pennsylvania, with branches in New Jersey and Delaware. Mr. Jessup lives in Pennsylvania but works across the state line in Delaware. Last year when his mother was terminally ill Mr. Jessup took 10 weeks of unpaid leave to care for her. This year Mr. Jessup was in a car accident while driving the agency van on his way home from transporting clients from a day program. The van was parked at his house since his hours for agency driving are very irregular, and he has to respond to emergencies. Mr. Jessup cannot return to work for 3 months. When he does return he is physically disabled and limited in his ability to assist passengers into the vehicle.

To evaluate this situation, the managerial supervisor needs to know if the accident is work related and if the driver is entitled to Worker's Compensation? Since Worker's Compensation is state law, the location of Mr. Jessup's office (in this case, the state of Delaware) will be the critical factor in determining benefits.

If it is determined that the accident was not work related, it is important to know the agency's sick leave policies and how they are tied to the Family Medical Leave Act (FMLA) of 1995. Mr. Jessup may be entitled to further leave under the FMLA. However, since 10 weeks have already been taken, it is important to determine if this time is within that year since the FMLA limits the leave to a maximum of 12 work weeks within a 12-month period.

On Mr. Jessup's return, the agency will need to evaluate whether he can continue in his previous job. Here, the ADA would be applicable. Title I of the ADA requires employers of 15 or more employees to provide reasonable accommodation to employees with disabilities who can perform the essential functions of the job, unless it would impose an "undue hardship" requiring significant difficulty or expense. Under the ADA, the definition of disability encompasses individuals (1) having physical or mental impairments that substantially limit one or more major life activities, (2) having records of such impairments, or (3) who are regarded as having such impairment. A major life activity is any activity that an average person can perform with little or no difficulty, such as speaking, breathing, performing manual tasks, seeing, hearing, learning, caring for oneself, sitting, standing, lifting, reading, or working. In Mr. Jessup's case, a determination should be made if his disability qualifies him for consideration under ADA.

If Mr. Jessup is a qualified individual under ADA, then reasonable accommodations, such as restructuring the nonessential functions of the job or granting a modified work schedule, should be made. If, however, his disability, even with accommodations, prevents him from performing essential functions such as driving the vehicle or assisting passengers into the vehicle, the employer is not required to retain Mr. Jessup in this position. Mr. Jessup's employer is not required to create an entirely new position to accommodate Mr. Jessup, but the ADA does mandate that employers consider certain forms of a modified work program such as transferring a disabled employee to an existing, vacant position or to a permanent or reserved light duty position.

The FMLA and the ADA, which are both applicable in Mr. Jessup's case, complicate the issue of granting leave. Employers may be required to extend leave beyond the 12 weeks required by the FMLA as a form of reasonable accommodation under ADA. The ADA allows an indeterminate amount of leave as a reasonable accommodation barring undue hardship to the employer. A supervisor should seek assistance from agency human resource personnel, federal enforcement agencies including the EEOC, and the Department of Labor, Office of Federal Contract Compliance Programs (OFCCP), or state and local fair employment practices agencies.

THE LEGAL CONTEXT OF SEXUAL HARASSMENT

Sexual harrassment in the workplace has taken on added meaning in the last decade as employers and employees alike have recognized the full implications of such actions. We now turn to the case of Ms. Taylor and examine the issues of sexual harassment and privacy with which every managerial supervisor needs to be familiar.

Ms. Taylor was recently hired to work nights in a previously all male unit in a drug rehabilitation center. There is a common lounge shared by all the employees. On the bulletin board are a number of notices. Frequently people post cartoons, jokes, and other humorous items. Ms. Taylor notices a number of cartoons that are sexually explicit and crude. The men joke with each other frequently and often tell sexist and sexual jokes. As a newcomer and the first women in the unit, Ms. Taylor feels that she needs to go along to get along, so she never objects.

Mr. Brooks, another counselor, asks Ms. Taylor for a date after she has been working at the center for a month. She declines, and he persists. Finally, Ms. Taylor firmly tells Mr. Brooks that she is not interested and that his repeated requests make her feel uncomfortable. The other men begin to tease Ms. Taylor about her refusal of Mr. Brooks' advances. Ms. Taylor asks the men to stop the teasing, but they continue. Ms. Taylor continues to endure this treatment, which escalates to the men accusing her, in very lewd and explicit language, of encouraging Mr. Brooks.

Finally, when Ms. Taylor receives an obscene E-mail message, she notifies her supervisor, Mr. Anderson. Mr. Anderson meets with Mr. Brooks, tells him to stop his unwelcome solicitation of dates and his other communication with Ms. Taylor, and suspends him for 3 days for violation of the agency's sexual harassment policy. Mr. Brooks claims that he and Ms. Taylor are having a consensual romantic relationship and that it is no one else's business. He also states that his right to privacy is being invaded since his E-mail messages are private communications to Ms. Taylor.

The rehabilitation center has the legal responsibility to investigate Ms. Taylor's complaint, which may be an example of what is legally defined as a hostile environment of sexual harassment. Unwanted and repeated requests for dates and sexual conduct of a verbal and visual nature, such as the behaviors described in this case, all constitute sexual harassment.

Harassment on the basis of sex is a type of discrimination and is a violation of the Civil Rights Act of 1964 and of state and local laws. According to Title VII of that act, sexual harassment is defined as

Unwelcome sexual advances, requests for sexual favors, and other verbal or physical conduct of a sexual nature when:

1. Submission to such conduct is made either explicitly or implicitly a term or condition of an individual's employment;
2. Submission to or rejection of such conduct by an individual is used as the basis for employment decisions affecting such individuals; or

3. Such conduct has the purpose or effect of unreasonably inter-
fering with an individual's work performance or creating an in-
timidating, hostile, or offensive work environment.

Demanding sexual favors in return for hiring, promotion, salary
increase, or any work-related condition as defined in points 1 and
2 above is termed quid pro quo sexual harassment. Although the
most blatant form of sexual harassment, quid pro quo situations
are less common than the hostile environment type defined by
point 3 and illustrated by our case example. The Supreme Court
has ruled in *Forklift v. Harris, 1993*, that a victim of sexual harassment can recover damages if he or she can prove the workplace environment was abusive to a reasonable person. The Court
also held that the victim does not have to prove individual psychological harm. Severe or pervasive conduct can lead to a hostile environment.

The EEOC issued policy guidelines defining sexual harassment
and establishing employer liability. Guidance is provided for the
following:

- Determining whether sexual conduct is "unwelcome";
- Evaluating evidence of harassment;
- Determining whether a work environment is sexually "hos-
  tile";
- Holding employers liable for sexual harassment by supervi-
  sors; and
- Developing preventive and remedial action.

An effective preventive response by the employer in Ms. Taylor's case should include a policy prohibiting sexual harassment
and internal complaint procedures by which employee allegations
of sexual harassment may be promptly addressed in a confidential manner. Effective remedies include protecting victims and wit-
nesses from retaliation, and taking appropriate corrective action
to end the harassment. Restoring lost employment benefits or opportunities, prevention of a recurrence of the misconduct, and
disciplinary action against the offender, ranging from reprimand

to discharge, are among the actions an employer should take. Training for employees and supervisors on the organization's policy and procedures as well as sensitivity to what behaviors may constitute sexual harassment are important components of a proactive response.

In our case, Mr. Anderson acted appropriately in disciplining Mr. Brooks, assuming that an investigation found Ms. Taylor's allegations to be credible. If Mr. Anderson ignored, tolerated, or condoned the complaint, he would be jeopardizing the agency and encouraging Ms. Anderson to take the matter to an outside state or federal agency such as EEOC. An employer is liable if he or she knew or should have known of the harassment.

Mr. Anderson should seek advice on how to handle this situation from an appropriate human resource professional and/or his supervisor before proceeding. Some employers require formal reporting and investigations of sexual harassment complaints to ensure that prompt, unbiased, and consistent actions are taken by knowledgeable and trained professionals. It is also important that there be an institutional record of the incident and the remedy. Employees should have an option of reporting sexual harassment to someone other than their direct supervisor.

When discipline is being issued, particularly in a union workplace, it is important that there be consistency so that there are no violations of union contracts, work rules, or policies and procedures that could lead to allegations of unfair labor practices. Mr. Anderson and the rehabilitation center should also take actions to educate the men involved in the other harassing acts, such as the jokes and comments to Ms. Taylor, and to stop their conduct. A policy and procedure for sexual harassment complaints should be disseminated to all employees and appropriate training should be offered. The center should make clear that hostile environment sexual harassment includes unwelcome sexual advances, requests for sexual favors, and other verbal, visual, or physical conduct of a sexual nature, including messages sent via E-mail, voicemail, fax, etc. Mr. Brook's repeated requests for dates and his obscene E-mail message are creating a hostile environment and are not protected by privacy laws.

THE LEGAL CONTEXT OF EMPLOYEES' RIGHT TO PRIVACY

Employees' rights to privacy have also become an important issue, as illustrated in Ms. Taylor's case. Work policies and procedures need to balance the right of an employer to obtain and use information about prospective and current employees with their privacy rights. With E-mail and other technology available, these issues have become more complex. Thus although the right of an employer to read employees' E-mail messages generated on the employer's computer system has become a controversial issue, E-mail correspondence at the workplace is ordinarily not considered to be a private matter. The Electronic Communications and Privacy Act, 18 U.S.C. et seq., generally prohibits the interception of E-mail messages except for the person or entity who supplies the E-mail system.

An employee sued his employer who had discharged him after reading several E-mail message he had sent to his supervisor. In the case, *Smyth v. Pillsbury Co.*, 914 F Supp. 97 (E.D. Pa 1996), the employee sued for wrongful discharge, alleging that his termination violated Pennsylvania's public policy in favor of the right to privacy. The employer discharged the employee for transmitting inappropriate and unprofessional comments over the E-mail system, such as a threat to "kill the back-stabbing bastards," referring to sales management. The court denied the employee's claim, finding that employees have no reasonable expectation of privacy in their E-mail messages and that employers' interception of E-mail messages is not a substantial and highly offensive invasion of privacy (Ballard, Spahr, Andrews, & Ingersoll, 1997). The court further noted that the company's interest in preventing inappropriate and unprofessional comments or illegal activity over its E-mail system outweighs any privacy interest the employee may have in E-mail comments.

In our sexual harassment case, the E-mail message was shared with the supervisor by Ms. Taylor who found it offensive. The supervisor, Mr. Anderson, did not intercept the E-mail message, but even if he had done so, it is not likely that the communication would have been protected by privacy laws.

Employees should be put on notice that their E-mail communications are subject to interception. An E-mail policy should be distributed that clearly states the employer's right to review, store, and disclose all information sent over the system. The policy should specifically prohibit illegal and improper use such as pornography, obscenity, harassment, and gambling. Employees should be advised that even deleted messages can be retrieved. Other employer policies should be revised to address the use of E-mail. Sexual harassment via E-mail should be explicitly prohibited in the sexual harassment policy (Fox, Rothschild, O'Brien, & Frankel, 1997).

THE LEGAL CONTEXT OF VIOLENCE IN THE WORKPLACE

Workplace violence or abuse takes many forms. In the situation with Ms. Taylor and Mr. Brooks, sexual harrassment was involved. In other situations, physical violence and emotional abuse occur (Bray, 1995). We now turn to a situation in which a supervisory manager faces issues of workplace violence or abuse.

Nathan Jones receives a complaint from a patient about Delores Smith, a hospital social worker whom he supervises. The patient alleges that Ms. Smith became argumentative and belligerent when she complained about Ms. Smith's delay in returning her calls. The patient demands that a different social worker be assigned to her. She does not want Ms. Smith to know she has complained because she is fearful that Ms. Smith will retaliate and react violently.

Ms. Smith has been a competent social worker until the last 6 months. Following the death of her mother, Ms. Smith has been absent and late on many occasions. Her reports have not been of the same high quality that they were in the past. Other social workers have alerted Mr. Jones that Ms. Smith has mood swings, seems depressed and unhappy some days, and is hyperactive and cheery on others. One of Ms. Smith's coworkers also tells Mr. Jones that she suspects Ms. Smith is on drugs.

Mr. Jones is reluctant to confront Ms. Smith, hoping that all she needs is some time to grieve and recover from her mother's death. But since it has been 6 months and the problems are escalating, Mr. Jones calls Ms. Smith into his office and begins to tell her that her attendance, lateness, and quality of work are not acceptable. Ms. Smith reacts angrily to Mr. Jones and threatens to get back at him, her coworkers, and the entire hospital for its lack of compassion for her during her time of mourning her mother. She threatens to go to her union over his harassment of her and then leaves his office, slamming the door behind her.

At this point, Mr. Jones should immediately consult with his supervisor and labor relations professionals at the hospital. The possibility and threat of a violent reaction by Ms. Smith should be taken seriously. Quick action is needed to obtain assistance for her and remove her from the workplace where she may harm patients or other employees. This employee is the type who should be referred to an Employee Assistance Program or other professionals who assist employees whose personal problems are affecting their work performance. The hospital has the right to require the employee to take a leave of absence to recover from the problems that may be affecting her, including drug or alcohol use.

The Occupational Safety and Health Administration (OSHA) requires that employers protect their employees from a violent environment including attacks by clients, coworkers, strangers, and people they know. Courts have also ruled that employers must take corrective measures to safeguard other people when they either know or should have known that an employee is dangerous.

A first step in eliminating violent or abusive behavior in the workplace is to develop a clear definition of what is unacceptable behavior. Bray (1995) contends that this is important for three reasons. First, having a written statement of what constitutes abusive behavior assists employees in knowing when they have been treated inappropriately. This is clarification for employees and the written statement can provide a standard for behavior. Second, it is often hard to distinguish between what is appropriate criticism in the workplace and when someone has crossed over the line. Since managerial supervisors are constantly providing feedback, they and their employees need to know what constitutes abuse and what is considered appropriate feedback needed for improving a worker's job performance. Conversations about what constitutes appropriate and inappropriate behavior is a way to open communication on the topic.

Third, some persons may be looking for reasons that address why their performance in the workplace is not adequate. Eliminating abuse as the cause may lead to their getting help with whatever the real problem is. Bray puts it this way: "refusing to name a certain experience as abusive does not deny that the person who had the experiences is in pain. The pain can be acknowledged, even though the cause of it may not be abuse" (Bray, 1995, pp. 87–88). In the case of Ms. Smith it is important for Mr. Jones to recognize that Ms. Smith feels as if she has suffered from a lack of compassion in the workplace, given her mother's death. Being aware of these perceptions is important in defining what has happened. Employees often have expectations of their work environments that cannot possibly hold up under stress. If Ms. Smith expected the workplace to provide a safe environment in which she could grieve, her expectations were unrealistic.

Employers can take a number of preventive steps in addressing violence in the workplace. These include

- teaching employees dispute resolution techniques;
- upgrading security systems;
- offering seminars on safety, domestic abuse, and crime prevention;
- making sure employees know that any fighting, threats, violence, or possession of a weapon at work is cause for immediate discharge; and
- implementing an Employee Assistance Program (EAP) so that workers can get help for any emotional, drug, alcohol, or similar problems that could trigger violent reactions.

Managerial supervisors will want to be proactive in taking some or all of the steps listed above. When a violent or abusive episode occurs, employees will be highly stressed and fearful. Having policies in place and having had discussions about how an episode will be handled before anything happens are critical. Once an episode has occurred, it is important for the manager to review the situation carefully and quickly so that employees have confidence that their work environment is protected.

The Legal Context of the
Termination Period

The following two cases have been selected because they deal with a respected employee who must be terminated for reasons unrelated to previous job performance as well as with an employee who is being terminated because of poor performance. Both situations raise important issues for the supervisory manager to consider.

Termination due to Disability

Mr. Jessup, the van driver whose case was previously discussed, has returned to the agency and it is clear that he cannot continue in his previous position because of his physical handicap. Mr. Jessup is given a temporary position while management, together with union officials, explore all possible options to retain Mr. Jessup. The agency is undergoing cutbacks and several of the branch offices will be closed; furthermore, the board of directors is exploring a merger with another agency. The only position available is a technical one in the accounting department for which Mr. Jessup has no qualifications. In addition, two people from the branches that are being closed are qualified for this position. The agency offers to help Mr. Jessup seek work elsewhere and also offers to pay for a retraining program in an area that he could handle.

The ADA was designed to protect persons with disabilities, [such as Mr. Jessup], in both their seeking and retaining work. At the same time the policy recognizes that some situations require flexibility in the adjustments to be made. The ADA permits an employer to require that an individual not pose a direct threat to the health and safety of the individual or others in the work place. A direct threat means a significant risk of substantial harm. You cannot refuse to hire or fire an individual because of slightly increased risk of harm to himself or others. Nor can you do so based on a speculative or remote risk. The determination . . . must be based on objective, factual evidence regarding the individual's present ability to perform essential job functions. If . . . an employee poses a direct threat . . . , you must consider whether the risk can be eliminated or reduced to an acceptable level with a reasonable accommodation. (U.S. Equal Opportunity Commission, BK 17, 1991, p. 14)

It is clear that Mr. Jessup would present a risk to the passengers in the van, a risk that cannot be eliminated or reduced. In preparation for termination, he can be helped to apply to his state's Department of Employment Security for Unemployment Compensation while, at the same time, he can be helped to re-tool or retrain, as well as to find other work. He may also be eligible for disability insurance if he has this coverage. The health benefits under COBRA (the federal law requiring that terminated employees be offered continued health coverage if they elect to pay for it) should also be explored.

This situation is a very difficult one because it is not Mr. Jessup's fault that he has acquired a disability. His fine work as a van driver and his good record over 15 years are respected in the agency. The managerial supervisor will want to work closely with Mr. Jessup so that this transition is as easy as possible.

However, there are situations in which termination is based on factors within the employee's control. We now turn to a case in which termination is due to incompetence.

Termination due to Incompetence

Ms. Gray is a social worker employed by a senior center. Although never a stellar worker, Ms. Gray's performance is adequate and all her performance evaluations are positive. Lately, her performance, particularly her recordkeeping and report writing, has been poor. All social workers are required to use a new computer program for compiling statistics, keeping records, and generating reports. Despite training and individual coaching and counseling, Ms. Gray refuses to use the new system.

Ms. Young has recently been promoted to be Ms. Gray's supervisor. The center director tells Ms. Young that Ms. Gray must begin to use the computer system as all other social workers are required to do. Ms. Young meets with Ms. Gray to tell her of the expectation and to offer her assistance in learning the system. Ms. Gray refuses, saying that her way of recordkeeping and report writing had been permitted by her former supervisor and if Ms. Young does not like it, she can fire her. Ms. Young realizes that things are getting heated and tells Ms. Gray that they will continue the discussion tomorrow. Later that day, while reviewing some past travel expense forms, Ms. Young discovers that there are some fraudulent expense forms that have been submitted by Ms. Gray.

When Ms. Young meets with Ms. Gray the next day, she questions her about the travel forms. Ms. Gray admits that she made up some travel since she "was a little short of cash and felt the center owed me the money since I am always laying out some of my own money to buy supplies for the center." After conferring with the center director, Ms. Young fires Ms. Gray. But she has not been told explicitly why she is being fired.

As Ms. Gray gathers her personal belongings, she tells a secretary that she has been fired because the center believes that she is too old to do her job. "How ironic," she says, "that there should be such ageism at a senior center." Ms. Gray claims that she overheard her supervisor say, "You can't teach an old dog new tricks. I wish Ms. Gray would realize that it's time for her to retire."

Ms. Gray was fired because she had violated a work rule and committed an illegal act. Under a progressive discipline system, which ranges from counseling to discharge, Ms. Gray's fraudulent expense report is likely to be a terminable offense. This case illustrates a number of issues that should be considered in managing a worker's performance and implementing discipline for a poor performer. The discharge of an employee, particularly one from a protected class, is a frequent cause for litigation.

Appropriate Steps to Be Taken

The following practices can help protect an employer from a wrongful discharge suit.

PROVIDE A FORMAL PERFORMANCE EVALUATION SYSTEM.   Candid, objective, and periodic performance evaluations are an effective means of keeping employees regularly advised of how they actually stand and of preventing future surprises. However, a performance evaluation that fails to address performance limitations and accurately state deficiencies, or that is merely perfunctory and does not inform an employee of how she or he is actually doing, can do more harm than good. Ms. Young has inherited a worker who believes her performance, as evaluated by her former supervisor, has been satisfactory and this by itself may have made it difficult for Ms. Young to manage Ms. Gray's performance. The longer poor performance is tolerated or ignored, the more difficult it is to take action and the greater the possibility that when an action is taken, especially with an older worker, a claim of discrimination will be made.

PROVIDE PROGRESSIVE DISCIPLINE AND DOCUMENTATION. A progressive discipline system, usually ranging from counseling to discharge for infractions of a shared set of work rules, allows the supervisor to enforce performance standards and to sanction appropriately. If the only problems with Ms. Gray are her report writing and failure to learn and use the computer system, Ms. Young should begin by counseling Ms. Gray about the expectations for her reports and the use of the computer. In this counseling session, the consequences of not improving report writing and recordkeeping should be clearly stated. Ms. Young should document the counseling session and then follow-up to see that improvements occur. If performance remains a problem, the next step in discipline should be taken. In this case, Ms. Gray's attitude and reluctance to learn to use the computer would likely require Ms. Young to take the next step and eventually to terminate the employee, even if the expense report incident had not come to light.

AVOID STATEMENTS THAT COULD BE INTERPRETED AS DISCRIMINATORY. Ms. Young's alleged statement alluding to Ms. Gray's age can increase the center's liability for a lawsuit on the basis of age discrimination. All supervisors should guard against statements and actions that are based on stereotypes and prejudices. The agency should be sure that its disciplinary practices and performance requirements do not discriminate against people on the basis of age, race, gender, disability, or any other protected class.

The Age Discrimination in Employment Act (ADEA) was originally passed into law in 1967 and was amended in 1978 and 1986 to protect workers 40 years of age and older from unfair discrimination at work. The number of charges filed with EEOC has been on the rise, and terminations of older workers are resulting in lawsuits. One of the reasons for this increase is inadequate documentation of poor performance (Cleveland & Shore, 1996, p. 636). In Ms. Gray's case previous supervisors did not document poor performance, which put the burden of proof on Ms. Young.

CONDUCT THE TERMINATION CONFERENCE PROFESSIONALLY AND CONFIDENTIALLY. Ms. Gray's firing should take place promptly and in private. The reason for the termination decision and any benefits the employee is entitled to receive or not receive should be explained clearly and concisely. Ms. Young should not argue or apologize for the decision. Since Ms. Gray's travel record falsification is likely to be considered gross misconduct, she can be excluded from COBRA coverage and unemployment compensation. It is important that a review procedure be available within the organization.

CONCLUSIONS

The cases offered here illustrate the complex nature of employment laws and regulations and the high risk of litigation in the event of mishandling personnel practices. Managerial supervisors should confer with human resource and labor law experts in their organizations before taking action, and they should be mindful that laws and regulations are subject to change. The purpose of providing some insight into handling personnel problems is to alert supervisors to be cautious before taking any actions and to consult with authorities.

There are resources available at all governmental levels. The United States Department of Labor and the Equal Employment Opportunity Commission can offer assistance. State and local governmental agencies, such as the Human Relations Commission, may also be consulted. Attorneys specializing in employment law are another valuable resource, as are workshops conducted by nonprofit support centers.

It is clear that managerial supervisors must be well informed of the agency's procedures in regard to the broad array of legal issues. It is equally clear that all human service agencies must not only have clear policies and practices in place, but must also be sure that these are clearly understood by all of the professional staff. Since the information is complex and the consequences of incorrect behavior are enormous, the availability of consultants and legal experts is a sine qua non for effective supervision in human service agencies.

The managerial supervisor must be sensitive to the organizational, professional, and personal elements of the situation. Since the supervisor is the linchpin between the organization and the front-line worker, this squarely provides a responsibility and creates an opportunity for effective supervision. It is important, however, that adequate processes are in place in the agency that provide the employee with protection from unreasonable administrative actions. Related matters are the subject of Chapter 9.

3

Building Strategic Alliances

In the past decade there has been a proliferation of partnerships among human service organizations. These relationships range from simply cosponsoring of events, through sharing staff and program resources, to structural integration. In this chapter we explore the role of managerial supervisors in the formation of all types of strategic alliances.

As managerial supervisors participate in alliance development, management, oversight, and even termination, they face an inevitable paradox. We view this paradox as one of allegiance: *Just as persons are responsible to the agencies in which they are employed and these agencies are often competitive with others, they are also often committed to alliances that are interorganizational and collaborative in nature.* As long as the goals of an employing organization are compatible with those of the alliance, things may work well to the benefit of both. However, there will always be times when it is necessary to step back and assess your allegiances, as alliances take new directions and your agency may actually be competing for resources with other alliance members. Mizrahi and Rosenthal (1993) describe this as "the cooperation-conflict dynamic" (p. 15).

In working with alliances, managerial supervisors will also discover very quickly that alliances do not flow in a neat, linear fashion. In fact, it is our experience that the process of alliance building is highly iterative and nonlinear. This pattern requires managerial supervisors to live with a great deal of ambiguity as relationships ebb and flow.

Whether an alliance is a more loosely connected affiliation or a formally arranged legal entity (i.e., merger, consolidation), we believe that more and more interorganizational relationships will develop as human service organizations move into the twenty-first century. Remembering the complexity and rapidity of even a few of the environmental and professional challenges described in Chapter 1, it is easy to understand why now more than ever supervisory managers must work harder and smarter in developing strategic alliances that cross agency lines with the ultimate goal of enhanced services for clients.

This chapter begins with an example of alliance building. We refer to this example throughout the chapter as we define alliance, identify how different types of interorganizational alliances can be structured, and focus on how supervisory managers can skillfully work with and in human service alliances.

A large health care system in the southwestern United States was rapidly diversifying beyond its original acute care hospital base. As managed care penetration in the area increased, leaders within this system realized the importance of having more control over services provided along a full continuum of care. If health care was going to be responsive to patient needs, this system had to turn its attention to providing home and community-based services. It was more than obvious that the arena in which care would be provided had shifted, and hospitals were only places in which the most severe episodes of illness were treated. Disabled and older persons, many with chronic conditions, were largely treated in the offices and clinics of primary care physicians, and intervention and rehabilitation were likely to occur in the home care setting. This required hospital-based staff to rethink the way in which they conceptualized the community context. It also posed the challenge identified in Chapter 1 of how professionals balance their own identities with interdisciplinary relationships.

Maria Rodriquez was hired as the managerial supervisor of the newly established Elder Case Management Program as the system expanded its scope. The mandate she was given by the administrators of the Chronic Care Division, buried deep within the bureaucratic system, was to reach out to local physicians and to form alliances with their practices. If case management of clients was to be fully successful in a managed care environment, it was critical to assess and monitor geriatric patients early, before their conditions required expensive acute care hospital stays. Although this sounded like a compassionate and proactive idea, Maria was also politically astute. She realized that physicians were not always enamored with the large system in which she was positioned, particularly since this system was seen as "gobbling up" practices for their growing physician network. In fact, in some local practices she encountered open animosity. Not only did Maria have to supervise a cadre of geriatric case managers and support staff, but she was the system's representative to diverse physician groups in the community. The net result was clearly an expansion of her job.

As we examine the ways in which alliances are defined and developed, we will use Maria Rodriguez and the Elder Care Management Program to illustrate each concept. We hope that managerial supervisors will be familiar with other examples that illustrate these concepts as well.

WHAT IS AN ALLIANCE?

There are multiple definitions and perspectives on the meaning of the terms "coalition" and "alliance." Often they are used interchangeably in the literature. For our purposes, however, we choose the word alliance in this chapter because we believe that relationships (whatever they are called) between various organizations must be sustained and that even as these partnerships change and new issues emerge, alliances imply the willingness to engage in ongoing relationship building in local communities. Alliance, then, is seen as an umbrella concept under which multiple types of interorganizational relationships can occur. Alliance implies that organizations will want to sustain these relationships, even though they will change over time. These relationships, obviously, take multiple forms and no two are exactly alike. This makes them interesting and challenging for anyone who is trying to participate in their formation, development, and maintenance. Managerial supervisors will find themselves engaging in these partnerships as they transcend organizational boundaries and interface with other community agencies in order to improve interorganizational collaboration and to reduce duplication of services.

In our case example, Maria Rodriguez quickly realized that the persons with whom she worked held multiple views of what an alliance could be. She knew that she needed to form lasting relationships with physician practice groups in the larger community, so that continuity of care would be provided, not just to patch together short-term coalitions. She wondered how to go about building these alliances.

Albrecht and Brewer (1990) distinguish between the terms coalition and alliance. Seeing traditional coalitions as groups that come together around certain issues that are addressed in a particular time frame, coalition participants are often viewed as temporarily engaging and then returning to their own members' agendas. They suggest that to truly collaborate, it is necessary to move beyond this view of coalition building and "see the concept of alliance as a new level of commitment that is longer-standing, deeper, and built upon more trusting political relationships. . . . coalitions [may be] short term solutions and alliance formation [becomes] ongoing, long-term arrangements for more far- reaching structural change" (p. 4).

WHY BUILD ALLIANCES?

Just as definitions of human service alliances differ, reasons for forming these entities are equally broad. It is useful to understand

the primary motivators underlining human service alliances because these perspectives offer guidance for creating alliances and
are also instructive for supervisory managers in maintaining them
(Gray & Wood, 1991).

MAXIMIZING RESOURCE DEPENDENCE
AND INTERDEPENDENCE

The most obvious prime mover behind the flurry of interorganizational activity among human service organizations is *resource dependence and interdependence.* Whether one of the prospective partners needs to depend on the resources of (an)others or all
recognize the synergistic potential in combining resources, the
underlying focus here is on maintaining and/or acquiring additional resources.

The issue of resource dependence and interdependence is often primary in an agency's decision to form an alliance that expands current services. For example, a human service organization may want to create an HIV/AIDS awareness program for
youth, but it may not be able to obtain funding for this purpose.
The only option may be to form an alliance with other local agencies such as health clinics or schools that have funding for
HIV/AIDS prevention activities and desire to reach a broader
population. Jointly these organizations can coordinate a program
that provides each agency with additional resources in support of
its own organizational objectives. The initiating agency would contribute access to a target audience and space for implementing
the program. The other member organizations would provide the
staff and educational materials to carry out the activities. In such
an example, full implementation of the program relies on the dependence and interdependence of all participating human service organizations.

In the case of Maria's Elder Case Management Program, the
concept of resource interdependence was definitely a driving
force. Health care systems are dependent on physicians for referrals and physicians want practice privileges in reputable local
facilities. Maria served as a vital link between the health care system and physician practices, and the case managers in her unit

were persons responsible for resource planning for older persons. Resources, and controlling the cost of these resources, served as a mutually motivating force between this health care system and local physicians. Even with their differences, everyone could agree that if they did not manage resources well, neither the health care system nor physician practices would survive.

INCREASING OPERATIONAL EFFICIENCY

Another important factor operating in today's human service partnering is *operational efficiency*, the focus of which is maximizing available resources by increasing organizational efficiency in service delivery and/or on-going operations. The Elder Case Management Project was definitely viewed as a way of maximizing efficiency. Case management, by definition, is an attempt to orchestrate and streamline service delivery in a way that consumers may not be able to do themselves. What Maria faced, as a supervisory manager, was the conflict this push toward operational efficiency presented—how would case managers balance advocacy with cost containment? With no easy answer to this question, Maria knew that she would be the person to whom case managers turned when they felt that the system in which they worked was more concerned about cost savings than advocating for patient needs.

Another example of the push for operational efficiency is "one-stop shops" such as Family Resource Centers. These service consortia are created to increase the efficiency of service delivery to clients in a geographic area by offering a continuum of services to clients (e.g., child care, child welfare, job training, and medical services) in one location with a single access point. Colocation of these agencies streamlines client referral processes. Moreover, the creation of an alliance to coordinate this effort allows member agencies to allocate various operational expenses across all member agencies rather than be held singly responsible for them. In some cases, the alliance may jointly lease a building and necessary equipment and hire the required staff to centralize various administrative tasks, which also promotes operational efficiency.

ACHIEVING STRATEGIC ENHANCEMENT

Achieving a competitive advantage or *strategic enhancement* is a more recent phenomenon among human service organizations, largely stimulated by the movement of for-profit organizations into the provision of social services. The issue of organizational survival is at the core of this movement, and the assumption is that organizations form alliances in order to gain a market edge.

For example, Maria quickly discovered that an organization's participation in a managed care network, frequently motivated by an overriding concern for agency survival, is a good example of strategic enhancement. Human service organizations may join managed care networks in the short term to compensate for reductions in funding, or they may be concerned about long-term survival as managed care contracts continue to account for an ever increasing portion of revenue. Regardless of an organization's time horizon, participation in a managed care network for these reasons potentially strengthens the human service organization's position to remain viable in an increasingly competitive service delivery environment by diversifying its funding sources, broadening its client base, and enhancing information and evaluation systems.

SEEKING ENVIRONMENTAL VALIDITY

Another newly recognized need among human service organizations is *environmental validity*. Alliances are formed to maintain and, hopefully, increase each member organization's legitimacy within its stakeholder group. With the rise of competition for vital resources (including qualified personnel) and the growing number of health and social concerns, human service providers must work harder to maintain the quality of service delivery needed to keep their level of credibility and hold the attention of caring stakeholders.

Alliances, such as the one established with local physician practices by Maria's Elder Case Management program, are created to improve interdisciplinary collaboration and to reduce duplication of services. These types of alliances are examples of programs seeking to maintain environmental validity. In many cases these alliances are mandated by funders. The agency gains credibility with its funder by following through on the recommendation. If participation in the coalition is not a condition of funding, the agency may still hope to increase its legitimacy with future funders by demonstrating its willingness to cooperate with other stakeholders in the community. Likewise, the agency may intend to enhance its validity as perceived by professionals, thus increasing its visibility and capitalizing on the opportunity to highlight its commitment to addressing shared issues. In Maria's case, the health care system prided itself on its relationships with the larger medical community.

GAINING POLITICAL POWER

Political power is a newly appreciated factor in human service organizations as they negotiate and respond to their new environments. This is a reality in our case example.

Maria also realized that another motivator in her system was the desire for greater power and control. The health care system within which she was employed was attempting to position itself to be a continuing player in a rapidly changing field. Other systems were merging and acquiring smaller hospitals, and Maria's system already had five hospitals within its domain. In fact, with the way things were going, this system was likely to be the only nonprofit provider of health care in the city. She would be naive to believe that the alliance she was building with physician practices was not a part of a larger plan that included acquiring some of those physician practices as part of the growing physician network owned by her system.

Therefore, when she approached physicians and they expressed concerns about being "bought up," she could not guarantee that this would not happen. What she did realize is that she had to create a connection with these practices so that case managers could work effectively with clients, and this required being totally aligned with the primary care physicians who served older persons. She believed that her commitment to clients was her first allegiance, and this sealed the necessity of building partnerships with community-based physicians and their staff.

Movements toward service integration, as illustrated in what Maria was attempting to do, are reflections of the political rationale behind alliance building (Waldfogel, 1997). Attempts to increase organizational power can be examined in many human service mergers.

Consider, for example, the merger of a mid-sized child welfare organization with a job training agency, JOBS. The child welfare agency offers a wide range of direct services throughout the eastern half of the county. With federal, state, and local efforts focused on welfare reform, the child welfare agency seeks to increase its power to impact the larger child welfare agenda and to increase its service delivery area through organizational mergers. The JOBS Agency runs a small job training program on the west side of the county and is widely recognized for its research and evaluation capacity. JOBS is anxious to expand its research to examine welfare to work initiatives being developed countywide. The goals of both agencies are furthered through a merger that subsumes JOBS and creates a new division of the public child welfare agency that is focused solely on research and evaluation. The merger links the expanded child welfare agency with the employment program throughout the county and increases its power as an organization seeking to affect welfare reform in the state.

Increasing Social Responsibility

Human service organizations that are mission-laden entities formed to address societal issues (unlike their for-profit counterparts) are increasingly called on by the public to increase their level of *social responsibility*. This pressure often serves as a motivator in the formation of human service alliances.

Just as Maria was seeking to link her case managers with physicians who could refer vulnerable older persons, there are examples of this search for social responsibility across population groups at risk. For example, with increasing numbers of academically at-risk children nationwide, communities are becoming more vocal about the need to improve primary and secondary education. Consequently, human service organizations are linking with local schools, universities, and for-profit organizations to conduct research and provide comprehensive community support to children and families with the goal of raising academic performance. These alliances take many forms and include a wide range of services. In some instances, the roles of the member agencies in the educational enhancement efforts may not directly relate to their current service offerings. However, as in all social responsibility alliances, specific agency roles are part of an overall programmatic effort with the primary goal of responding to expectations for action in the area of public concern.

In sum, whether alliances are being built to serve at-risk children or vulnerable elders, there are many reasons why alliances are formed. Although supervisory managers may not be at the table when the agreements are made, sustaining these entities requires a level of skill that is best served by a foundation of knowledge of the whys and hows underlying the alliance. To do so, managerial supervisors may find it helpful to have an understanding of the different types of alliances. We now turn to ways in which alliances have been categorized.

TYPES OF INTERORGANIZATIONAL ALLIANCES

Interorganizational alliances vary in terms of how they may be structured and why they may be formed. To better understand these differences, we identify four basic forms that, although not exhaustive, represent a continuum of alliance types. Our typology is based on the degree of autonomy among the designated organizations (Bailey & Koney, 2000).

At one end of the continuum, as shown in Table 3.1, is the *affiliation*, a loosely connected system of two or more organizations with similar interests. In this type of alliance, member organizations remain independent, yet cooperate and influence one another through the dissemination of ideas and information. Maria's alliance with local physicians is an example of an affiliation. Physician practices were separate from the health care system, yet they agreed to link with each other because of similar interests—the need to provide case management to older persons.

Moving along the continuum there are the *federation/associations* and *coalitions* that mutually coordinate limited areas of operations. The federation/association usually has a staff office to centralize common functions, such as fundraising, public relations, and mission advocacy. Member organizations are largely in-

Table 3.1: Typology of Interorganizational Alliances

Type of Alliance	A. Objectives of Participating Organizations	B. Organizations' Degree of Autonomy	C. Managers' Skills
Affiliation	Self-interest of each organization is primary	Total	Recognition of differences and similarities between own human service organization and others
Federation/ association/ coalition	Achieving both own and alliance goals are joint	Moderate	Ability to align activities with other organizations
Consortium/ network/ joint venture	Partners' interests also recognized	Minimal	Ability to manage differences and build consensus
Merger/ acquisition/ consolidation	New objectives are defined	None	Ability to relinquish autonomy

dependent, but the federation often determines the members' roles and the allocation of resources through the development of policies. Coalitions are also comprised of independent organizations that most often share a political or social change goal. Coalitions may also have a central coordinating staff, yet each member organization retains its autonomy, making contributions to the whole based on its resources and expertise.

Consortia, networks, and *joint ventures* go beyond coordinating operations to more formally working together through collaboration. Members of a consortium, a partnership of organizations that identifies itself with a particular interest/issue domain, collectively apply their resources to implement a common strategy and achieve a common goal.

Consortia often adhere to a jointly composed letter of agreement and are frequently sponsored by convening organizations that take responsibility for the overall collaboration. The network, like consortia, also consists of organizations that share resources for mutual benefit; however, legal documents govern the specifics (the hows and whys) of this sharing. In networks members maintain their own identities and governing bodies (i.e., boards of trustees) and usually retain their core functions such as human resource management and finance. The joint venture is similar to the network in that there are legal ties involved. A joint venture is, in fact, a legally formed alliance in which member organizations maintain joint ownership (generally through a jointly formed governance body) to carry out specific services and tasks. Members do, however, retain their individual identities and governing bodies, but if one organization withdraws from this alliance the joint venture dissolves.

At the end of the continuum of this interorganizational typology are the *mergers/acquisitions* and *consolidations* wherein organizations unite to form an integrated structure. A merger/acquisition is a statutorily defined alliance in which one organization is totally absorbed by another. The absorbed organization is completely dissolved and the surviving entity acquires both its assets and liabilities. In a consolidation all original organizations are dissolved. In this interorganizational form two or more organizations come together to form a new organization. The assets and liabilities of the original organizations are combined, and a new unified governing board is created.

> In our case, the resistance Maria encountered, as she contacted physician offices and explained her new case management system, was largely based on physicians' concerns that they would literally be merged, acquired, or consolidated with the health care system in which she was employed. Maria felt frustrated by this since it was not within her domain to assure them that this would not happen. As a managerial supervisor she had a responsibility to her staff to pave the way as best she could for a strong alliance with local practices. How would she manage these relationships?

MANAGING ALLIANCES

Inherent in this typology of organizational alliances are the skills required by the managerial supervisor who either staffs or oversees the functioning of these human service alliances. What Maria faced is not unique. Although she worked within one organization and was not at a high administrative level, she still had to

balance her oversight of staff within the organization and her relationships with the alliance of physicians in the community. Table
3.1, Column C, describes the similarities and differences in managers' roles in facilitating the maintenance of these alliances.

Affiliations require managers to identify the areas of difference
and similarity, as well as mutual interests, between their own organizations and potential partners. These areas may be seen in
the operating systems and structure of the organizations or even
in their fundamental missions. Although the interests of one's
own human service organization are most important, the chance
to provide some form of support to another agency can be viewed
as an opportunity.

Managerial supervisors working with federations or coalitions
must be able to build on the areas of difference and similarity to
purposefully align their agencies' specific activities with those of
other human service organizations. Managers must be able to
wear "two hats"—that of their organization and that of the alliance—to achieve the commonly held goals of both.

In consortia, networks, or joint ventures, supervisors often
bring in a neutral mediator to ensure that the basic needs of all
are identified and, ideally, met. Managers must recognize that the
partnering agencies are necessary to the attainment of their own
goals. Still wearing "two hats," that of the organization and that
of the alliance, the managers must make the hat of the alliance
the most prominent one.

Managerial supervisors involved in forming mergers or consolidations must have the ability to see beyond their own agency's
self-interests and wear only the "hat" of the new entity. Despite
the input of a neutral third person, this is usually the most difficult role for managers, especially in western societies that value
individualism highly. Managing the morale of personnel is most
important here; most of the time mergers and consolidations result in reductions in force, while requiring those that remain to
take on a new organizational identity with concomitant adjustments to roles and responsibilities.

In Maria's case, she wondered exactly what type of strategic alliance she was forming. It was not enough to loosely affiliate with

physicians, for her case managers needed to share information systems, actually meet with physicians in staffings of older clients, and have access to confidential information. Maria's case managers were visiting in the homes of older patients, at the request of their physicians, yet the physicians did not see themselves as supervisors for case managers. Maria spent time going from practice to practice, visiting with physicians and their staff to set up appropriate protocols. This was becoming more than an affiliation, it was a long-term alliance. Yet, she had to be careful to deal with their concerns and fears about being absorbed by the system that she represented. She felt immense loyalty to the physicians and case managers as an interdisciplinary team, simultaneously wearing the "hat" of health care manager and the "hat" of alliance builder.

In addressing the morale and personnel issues faced by Maria and others in alliance building, Mizrahi and Rosenthal (1993) identify four dynamic tensions that are characteristic of such partnerships: (1) mixed loyalties, (2) autonomy versus accountability, (3) means versus goal, and (4) unity versus diversity. *Mixed loyalties,* as we have already illustrated, occur when managers have to balance the goals of their own organizations with those of the alliance. *Autonomy versus accountability* is faced by alliances as they amass power and attempt to pursue their goals, but must be responsible to those multiple member organizations that sustain them. *Means versus goal* can generate a crisis for alliance members if they cannot agree on their purposes. Is the alliance simply a means to achieve a cause or a mutually beneficial result, or is the alliance a model of sustained organizational coordination that is very process and relationship oriented?

The likelihood is that most alliances represent both outcomes and processes to their constituencies, but problems can arise when one receives priority over another and members disagree. Last, the existence of elements of both *unity and diversity* is the dynamic tension that makes alliances the fluid vehicles that they are. If one believes that there is strength in diversity, then alliances conceivably can draw incredible strength from their diverse members. On the other hand, finding ways to unify those diverse strengths for action takes skillful leadership. The supervisory manager, indeed, is in a position to practice what she or he already knows about team building among staff in the organization, and take those skills to a broader arena when participating as an agency representative in interorganizational alliance building.

LIFE CYCLES OF ALLIANCES

The life cycle of alliances is a critical area that requires the managerial supervisor's attention. As is true with all entities that evolve over time, interorganizational alliances can be understood by their phases of growth and regression (cf. the National Assembly of National Voluntary Health and Social Welfare Organizations, 1991; Roberts-DeGennaro, 1986, 1997; Rosenthal & Mizrahi, 1990; Synergos Institute, 1992). What follows is one model of development (Bailey & Koney, 1995).

The general life cycle of alliances consists of four stages, adapting the work of Tuchman and Jensen (1977): (1) assembling the member organizations, (2) ordering the alliance, (3) performing the task, and (4) ending the alliance. Each stage can be understood by describing the specific issues and transition themes.

Assembling

In *assembling*, the first phase of alliance formation, the leaderships of the potential partnering organizations come together to explore the possibility of an alliance.

This occurred for Maria when she had intense face-to-face conversations with physician office managers about what their organizations had in common. She knew that each office manager had to assess what her or his organization could gain from this relationship. Possible roles and responsibilities and conflicting loyalties between individual organizations and this new union were then explored. Ideally, when this assembling phase ended, Maria would have agreement from the office manager that physicians in that practice would form an alliance. However, not too surprisingly, she discovered that this is also the time when most alliances fail. She was not able to partner with six physicians in one group who were too wary of her employing organization to participate in the case management–physician alliance.

Ordering

Our case continues to be instructive as we explore the life cycle of alliances. The importance of the ordering step cannot be underestimated.

> When Maria did gain a commitment from a practice group, to at least tentatively work with her case management program, she knew she could move into the ordering phase. At this point discussions became intense, alternating from being politely formal and written to suddenly explosive when face to face. This level and type of emotionality coupled with a clearer sense of the benefits and costs of the alliance can cause some of the original members to leave. Fortunately, for Maria the five medical practices with which she was partnering did not leave at this point. Membership issues remained important as "the kinks" were worked out and as dialogues with new practices took place to ensure that the alliance could sustain itself and expand its base of resources over time.

It is important to emphasize that each step is important in setting the groundwork for an effective alliance.

Performing

> As potential conflicts were resolved with particular practices, Maria knew that she could then move to implementing the case management program within that practice setting. Her attention would then turn to the structure of the alliance. This meant establishing procedures and designing the program so that case managers would have ways to communicate with physicians and their staffs in as efficient a way as possible. During this phase the physician–case manager alliance began to reconcile desires for control with the need for inclusion of others. For example, what role would members of local human service organizations play in this alliance, since these agencies were often the providers of in-home care services. During this process, Maria was aware that mores were established that focused on decision making as well as managing consensus and conflict. These were not always stated, but emerged as norms as alliance members became more open and direct in their communication with one another.

In the *performing* phase, alliances turn their collective attention outward. Yet, to do so, all members must understand the costs and benefits of this relationship to their organizations, know how their organizational roles and responsibilities contribute to the success of the partnership, and concurrently pledge allegiance to the goals of union over and above their own goals. These actions are critical to executing the specific tasks of the alliance. With fewer official meetings, communications among partners tend to be written with the leader monitoring the effectiveness of the alliance's earlier defined systems, strategy, and structure. Opportunities for members to acknowledge progress and setbacks must be made and this information used to enhance relationships with others (individuals and organizations) outside of the alliance to support its work.

ENDING

The *ending* phase of any union is when the purpose of the alliance as originally conceived either changes or officially ceases to exist. This can occur when the agreed upon tasks are completed and the purpose is accomplished, when the tasks are not completed but everyone wants to end the relationship, or when the partnership stays together but changes its original mission, thus starting the life cycle over again. Particular attention during this time must be paid to sustaining communication among the members and the external supporters to formally assess the process and products of the alliance.

Maria's goal was to establish an ongoing affiliation with physician practices in the community, but she also knew that physicians would come and go, and that health care was rapidly changing. Some physicians did leave, meaning that she had to regain the trust of new physicians entering practices in transition. One physician group was bought by her hospital system, which meant that they became part of the physician network with which she had more leverage, since they were now within the same overall structure. Another physician group decided to hire its own case manager. She determined that this was a sign of success—that they had realized the benefits of this role enough to integrate case management into their practice, but it also meant that they left the alliance and worked more independently.

As is true with all developmental models, each phase of the alliance builds on a previous one; the evolution may actually include one or more returns to the same phase. Moreover, the phases do not necessarily correlate with the age of the alliance. For example, a change in the identified leadership or membership may force an older partnership to return to a previous phase where it again will need to manage issues similar to those faced by a more recently formed union.

UNDERSTANDING ALLIANCE COMPONENTS

The phases of alliance building immediately brings attention to eight major components of alliances: (1) leadership, (2) membership, (3) environmental linkages, (4) purpose, (5) strategy, (6) structure, (7) systems, and (8) tasks (Bailey & Koney, 1995). Alliance *leadership* describes the formal (legitimate) and emergent (informal) individuals and/or organizations who direct and monitor the alliance, especially when there are three or more partners. This leadership must be shared.

All other partners comprise the *membership*, the organizational and/or individual participants who work with the leader. Again, supervisory managers are sometimes alliance leaders and often are either part of the membership or oversee their organizations' representatives in the alliance. *Environmental linkages* are the relationships between the alliance and the external stakeholders. These stakeholders can be both organizations and individuals. The *strategy* of this interorganizational entity is the way it increases its market share.

The strategy is designed to facilitate the partnership's achievement of its purpose, its mission, and its overall goals and objectives. *Tasks* are the specific activities that, when enacted, collectively assist in accomplishing the purpose of the alliance. *Structure* is the way the tasks and the members and leadership are divided, whereas *systems* are the operating ties that hold the structure together, including mechanisms for effective information flow, resource allocation, planning, personnel management, and evaluation (Bailey & Koney, 1995, p. 605).

Within these seemingly simple components rests the paradoxical realities that must first be acknowledged and then managed by supervisory managers, whether they are part of the alliance's leadership/membership stakeholders or supervising those who are. As suggested by their definitions, these components are highly interconnected. Today's supervisory managers must, therefore, honor the interdependence among these components by recognizing that all must function effectively for the alliance to thrive and that a change in any one component impacts all the others. In sum, managers of effective alliances recognize that leadership, membership, linkages, strategy, tasks, purpose, structure, and systems coexist, working in true partnership with one another. Critical to the process is recognizing how the interalignment of components is purposefully created, yet maintained in a flexible way that allows for maximum adaptability.

CHALLENGES AND BENEFITS OF STRATEGIC ALLIANCES

Although most persons working with and in human service organizations would agree with the benefits of forming partnerships, it is critical that supervisory managers be able to articulate both the opportunities and threats of these relationships. Such awareness assists not only in assessing the appropriateness of assembling, but also in enabling managers to be more vigilant in optimizing the effectiveness of the alliance's core components and monitoring the impact of the alliance on their own organization throughout the development of the alliance.

OPPORTUNITIES FROM PARTNERSHIPS

There are many positive results from alliances, which can be made explicit as follows:

- Potential for making a greater impact (e.g., service delivery/advocacy by broadening the resource base);
- Creating a situation of "safety in numbers," especially when the purpose of the alliance focuses on areas perceived as controversial and/or the agency members may be working in highly volatile and threatening situations;

- Ability to work with other organizations with which an individual member would not usually work;
- Capacity to set new standards of behavior—e.g., determining the ethical underpinnings of partnerships and reinforcing the need for agency accountability to local communities and funders;
- Ability to network, even globally, through the use of computerized technology; and
- Learning from one another, sharing strategies that are successes and failures (Salzburg Seminar, 1997).

Maria learned that establishing connections with local physicians made all the difference for gaining access to older persons' homes. If an older patient's primary care physician spoke highly of a case management, that person was immediately willing to accept the case manager into their home. There was no discounting the importance of this legitimation. When controversial issues arose in the community, being able to count on strong relationships with physician practices was incredibly important to Maria. At one point, physicians joined with her employing organization in backing a bill before the legislature that would support parity in mental health services for elders.

THREATS CREATED BY ALLIANCES

There are also potential threats faced in alliance building:

- Tasks generally get accomplished more slowly than if enacted by a single organization;
- Needing to compromise at every phase of development;
- Potential for losing one's own identity and autonomy;
- Possibility of members stealing ideas of others;
- Acquiring even more and different constituencies to serve and better represent; and
- Potential for being coopted/corrupted by others in an effort to maintain membership in the alliance (Salzburg Seminar, 1997).

Maria also experienced a number of threatening situations. Things got really "bogged down" when she needed to have face-to-face meetings with practice managers on an on-going basis, just to maintain relationships. Eventually, they had to agree to hold more efficient meetings. Another threat occurred when the practice that hired its own case manager actually recruited one of Maria's best case managers out from under her. The downside to having demonstrated such high level competence was that she lost a valuable staff person to another organization.

Managerial supervisors will be well served to remember these pros and cons of strategic alliances and to add to these lists based on their own experiences. It is important that managers help the entire staff to develop and implement strategies for identifying possible threats and minimizing their impact on the alliance. Whether beginning to work as an affiliation or stabilizing a consolidation, managers need to be able to identify and work with the developmental phases that facilitate the evolution of alliance building. Moreover, supervisors who are skillful in differentiating among an alliance's core components will be able to recognize, handle, and teach others how to manage them. Armed with knowledge and skills, supervisory managers can ensure that the proliferation of alliances will not just continue, but that human service alliances will be more effective in meeting the needs of all who are served.

CONCLUSION

In the paradoxical contemporary environment, where competition and collaboration coexist and agencies compete for resources as much as they seek alliances, supervisory managers face multiple challenges and opportunities. Knowing that there are different ways in which alliances evolve allows the managerial supervisor to recognize that the affiliation of today may be the merger of tomorrow. Understanding that alliances have life cycles and components can provide a frame of reference for the supervisory manager who suddenly finds him or herself representing the agency in a strategic alliance. Recognizing the challenges, opportunities, and pitfalls of alliance building will enhance one's savvy within the contemporary human service arena where collaborations and partnerships are critically important to service integration in local communities.

4

Humanizing Technology

How many times have we heard statements such as "we use computers only for billing, we still do our progress notes by hand," "a laptop computer would be a barrier between me and the client," or "now that we have all this technology, nothing works!" The frustrations that accompany the technological age are familiar and everyone has their favorite story of trying to figure out whether something is a hardware or a software or a "peopleware" problem.

In this chapter we contend that a critical function the managerial supervisor must perform is to humanize technology. This does not mean that the supervisor is a "computer tech"; what it does mean is that she or he has the responsibility to work with others to make technological advances work for them. The paradox that accompanies this function is that *the process of humanizing technology can appear very dehumanizing.* Indeed, transitions in the technological age can feel threatening to employees who find some of the tasks they did by hand assumed by a piece of software, an inanimate disembodied "thing" that comes on disk or

CD, ready to install. The fear underlying this threat is that they will no longer be needed as computers perform more work, or that they cannot perform as well. In some cases this will be true, but that same software will require an operator to tell it what to do. Managerial supervisors, then, must convey to their work teams the importance of "getting up to speed" so that they are in control of what is done, rather than throwing their hands up in frustration when they do not understand the nuances of a new software program. There are roles for human beings in all of this, but they are not always the same roles played just a few years ago.

We begin this chapter by defining technology and providing an overview of the ways in which technology is changing the work lives of persons in health and human service organizations. Next we identify basic questions to ask in assessing one's technological needs. We then focus on the implications of new technologies for organizational practice in human services, followed by an examination of the problems encountered by supervisory managers as they deal with technological issues.

DEFINING TECHNOLOGY

"Technology" is a broad term that encompasses the techniques and procedures that professionals use in working with consumers of service. Years ago Hasenfeld (1983) defined human service technologies as "a set of institutionalized procedures aimed at changing the physical, psychological, social, or cultural attributes of people in order to transform them from a given status to a new prescribed status" (p. 111).

For example, case management can be viewed as a human service technology according to Hasenfeld's definition. Case management consists of a set of procedures—screening, assessment, care planning, resource mobilization, intervention, monitoring, and reassessment—aimed at transforming persons who need multiple services into clients who have these various needs met.

Such human service technologies are intended to be humane approaches to client-based change, but that assumes that the people using them do so in a responsible, sensitive, and caring manner. For example, the practice technology used by a social work clinician may be cognitive restructuring, which is essentially an approach to assist persons in reframing how they view situations. This type of technology is not as concrete or easy to replicate as the use of a software package on a desktop computer. Another example is one aspect of technology used in most interventions with older persons—the multidimensional functional assessment tool. These types of tools are being redesigned, standardized, and published on an on-going basis. To keep up to date with this technology, a human service worker might want to access a web site on the Internet that focuses on the latest tools for work with elders.

Human service workers use the technologies they have been taught on a regular basis, but do not always think of these interventions, protocols, tools, procedures, and approaches as "technological," even though they are. In this chapter we deal with some of the more managerial technologies that are invading the work environment of today. We want the reader to keep in mind that these technologies are ways to manage one's own work and to support and update the worker in using intervention technologies with clients.

TECHNOLOGICAL CHANGE AS ON-GOING

The tendency is to think of technological change as synonymous with computerization. Yet, technological change can arrive in multiple forms. One writer talks about the invention of the telephone and its impact on how office buildings were designed. "It took fifty to seventy-five years for researchers to acknowledge the ways in which the ordinary telephone allowed the creation of the city landscape and different physical layout of organizations" (Shulman, 1996, p. 362). Shulman contends that if the telephone had not been invented, architects would be designing buildings with fewer floors and wider staircases between floors so that scores of runners would be able to get messages from person to person faster. Similarly, the centralization of large operations was transformed by the telephone, allowing corporate officers to be located separately from other facilities and still be able to communicate with their employees across these physically dispersed locations.

Obviously, the telephone is a mainstay in the offices of the world and was only the beginning of a wave of technological advances. The point is that with each new invention comes change in how work is organized and how communication occurs. The position of "runner" was likely threatened by the invention of the telephone, just as the human secretary of yesterday is turning into the voicemail system and computer terminal on a person's desk today. This is the human price of technological advances, and managers need to understand the very real implications of these changes for employees.

Just as persons in older office buildings today complain about the archaic wiring of their phone systems and how that needs to change so that they can get on with the newer technology, there was likely a time when the debates around the water cooler centered on whether everyone should have their own phone. Hard to believe? Twenty years ago moving to a correcting selective type-writer was considered "advanced" technology. Just 10 years ago it would have been considered a "perk" to have a computer terminal at one's desk, and having one was something to be negotiated in the hiring process. Now it is an expectation if people are going to be able to fulfill their job responsibilities.

Just as few people think of the telephone as being a "hi-tech" item in a busy office setting, other technological changes have become part of the contemporary workplace. Fax machines, mobile phones, speakerphones, video conferencing equipment, presentational software and hardware, electronic mail (E-mail), and a host of other options are transforming the workplace. The concept of the virtual office finds more and more persons connected electronically (see for example Root, 1996), staring into a computer terminal at home, wearing their robes and slippers. These changes have incredible implications for how people communicate, how things get done, how work is structured, and how people feel about work.

ASSESSING TECHNOLOGICAL NEEDS

Given the rapid change in technology and the increasing number of options, it is easy to jump on the technological bandwagon without fully reflecting on what is needed. Supervisory managers will also inherit existing systems with their accompanying problems, so sometimes a previous supervisor will have jumped on the bandwagon for you. Regardless, it is important to take some time to carefully assess exactly what is needed. Instead of focusing on what is available, such as "we must have Internet access because everyone else does," focus on what the organization and the people in it need to do. This is what we mean by humanizing technology.

We believe that there are at least four areas that the supervisory manager must consider in attempting to assess technology needs: (1) facilitating the employee's ability to do the job, (2) enhancing consumer connections with the agency, (3) ensuring accountability, and (4) ensuring access to information.

FACILITATING THE EMPLOYEE'S
ABILITY TO DO THE JOB

Consider what persons within your unit or organization need to be able to do in order to efficiently and effectively relate to one another. Who needs to communicate with whom? Is it important to have everyone connected? Where are the current breakdowns in communication that need shoring up? And how can everyone who uses the new technology become involved in the decision-making process? If, for example, your agency services clients in their own homes and your team spends a good deal of time "in the field," how will they communicate? Pagers may be the technological intervention needed, perhaps with cellular phones. But pagers and mobile phones are only vehicles to enhance communication and they need to be selected for that reason. If your team covers a highly rural area, then cellular phones may be almost mandatory since there may be few places where people can stop to call the office when their pagers go off. In addition, one of the factors the agency may want to provide for is safety. For workers who travel rural countrysides or busy interstate highways, having a phone in the car may be a safety mechanism as well. Again, the intent is to use technology to humanize how the agency treats its employees. To maintain productivity levels and staff morale, agencies will need to establish norms regarding how to use these new methods of communication. For example, norms might focus on avoiding "spamming" persons over E-mail or abusing the use of pagers. The point is that the technology selected is a means to solve communication and safety problems, not a trendy end in itself.

A supervisory manager may be encouraging workers who would like to do their paperwork at home. For some persons this will be a choice that they prefer. With this option, however, comes the possibility that a worker may be physically absent when something important happens. Certainly a telephone is a communication link, but messages are often transmitted via E-mail in the office. The employee may determine that working at home is a wonderful tradeoff, but wants to be responsible in accessing E-mail. Having a home computer through which E-mail can be accessed may mean that she or he is connected and can retrieve messages periodically. Similarly, if there is an answering machine on the employee's desk at work, she or he can access messages from other locations without having to bother anyone at the office. Again, connections to E-mail and the answering machine at work are vehicles to maintain contact when out of the office. They serve important communication and accountability functions.

Enhancing Consumer Connections With the Agency

Assessing how workers relate to one another, receive basic information, and stay connected to the unit or agency in which they work may enhance employee satisfaction with what they do, but it is only the beginning. Workers can interrelate very nicely, without consumers feeling any of the same connection. The next questions to ask concern how consumers connect with the agency. Do consumers view the agency as user friendly or as inaccessible? Do consumers know how to get what they need? What barriers do consumers encounter?

In the examples just given, if employees are given permission to work at home on their paperwork, can consumers still access these workers? If not, then perhaps by solving one problem, the manager will have created another. If, on the other hand, a consumer can dial a direct office line for the worker and the worker can access the message through an answering machine and promptly return the call, then perhaps the system works well.

However, consumers may gain access to the agency only to find that the new sophisticated communications system is a major barrier. How many times have people dialed their banks, power companies, human service offices, and a myriad of other organizations only to find that there is a long listing of options if the caller has a touch-tone phone. Following the selection of buttons, there is another directory of numbers to punch, and then the person at that voicemail box is not there. This is not exactly a sensitive way in which to treat the consumers of service. It is efficient, but whether it is effective depends on the tenacity of the consumer.

Probably the most difficult part of humanizing technology, then, is trying to make appropriate changes that will facilitate the work without being insensitive to or discounting consumer needs. On the other hand, there are instances in which technology can actually be a great equalizer. Zeff (1996) talks about how physical disabilities disappear in cyberspace. "In cyberspace no one knows if a person is in a wheelchair, stutters, or is deaf. In cyberspace a person with chronic fatigue syndrome can work at a comfortable pace" (p. 2). Assistive technologies offer examples of how people's lives can be transformed. In this regard, technology is a vehicle not only for consumers, but also for employees with disabilities so that the work environment becomes accessible to them.

Ensuring Accountability

A growing literature can be found on the development of computer software and management information systems (MIS) to meet specific agency/program needs (see, for example, Caputo, 1986; Huber, Borders, Netting, & Kautz, 1997; Hoefer, Hoefer, & Tobias, 1994; McCready, Pierce, Rahn, & Were, 1996; Rock, Beckerman, Auerbach, Cohen, Goldstein, & Quitkin, 1995; Williams, Netting, & Engstrom, 1991). How to establish a centralized data collection system from different agency departments for quality assurance (Auslander & Cohen, 1992) and how to structure case records (Edwards & Reid, 1989) have been examined. Furthermore, aspects of information systems such as data collection, (Allen-Meares & Lane, 1990) and recordkeeping (Kagle, 1993) are found in the professional literature.

With the design of information systems comes a human response to change. And it is this human response that must be understood and addressed by the supervisory manager. Even persons who totally agree with the computerization of their systems will have moments of doubt in the process of installing new hardware and software to make it happen. Murphy and Pardeck (1992) caution us about some of the drawbacks in computerized systems. Persons who design data collection forms and systems must recognize that complex bits of information and tasks with clients must often be simplified and placed in generic categories in order to be used and measured in a system. Data are sometimes thought of as objective and scientific, when in actuality every data element selected is based on value choices. Semke and Nurius (1991) warn about "poor fit" that can occur when an information system does not fully meet the needs of the organization. A symptom of poor fit is employee resistance using the system.

So what does a manager do to prevent or redress situations in which team members resist using new technology? First, it is essential that the supervisory manager have a clear understanding of the system that is being put in place or has already been installed. If it does not make sense to the manager then there is something wrong. It may be that information vital to the work is not being collected or that the system is not user friendly. Whatever the reason, the manager needs a clear understanding of how the system works (or does not). Second, it is important to problem solve. If something is not working, why is that the case and what are the options? This problem-solving process can involve members of the work team so that concerns and frustrations are expressed. This is the human side of the system. Employees may sincerely want the work-saving abilities of technology, but system designers do not fully understand what these employees do. It is not just a matter of putting terminals on people's desks. It is a matter of knowing the work they do so well that the software makes them marvel at how quickly they can do something on screen that took much longer to do by hand.

This brings us to the problems of starting an information system. If it is viewed simply as a "management" information system, it will be seen as a tool of management. The direct practitioner, the person who comes face to face with consumers, needs to be a part of system development. Otherwise, information systems will be seen as a way to evaluate performance and to check up on the person's work rather than as a valuable clinical tool to facilitate work more efficiently. Information systems are used for a variety of purposes, with accountability usually cited first so that managers can describe their efforts and provide results to funding sources and other constituents. But equally important to the direct practitioner is how these data will be used by advocates to support change in a turbulent political climate. Information systems can be used as planning vehicles as well, providing information that assists in future policy change and program design. There is even a public relations function performed by well-designed information systems as reports are generated that illustrate what is happening to consumers and how to deal with political opposition (see, for example, Barzelay & Armajani, 1992; Love, 1990).

Just as there are accountability, design, planning, public relations, and political reasons for having well-designed information systems, managers must be constantly concerned with making systems user friendly to the persons who have to use them. Software may need to be fairly basic and simple so that persons who are unfamiliar with computers can use it. Overwhelming people with forms can result in their ignoring or even sabotaging tasks. For example, "toggling" past fields that will be used by some and not by others can lead to inaccurate and confusing data entry. Involving the persons who will use the system to test it at every stage, welcoming their feedback, and getting back to them about what has been done about the issues they raise will engage staff in the process. Staff ownership of these systems is necessary for their success.

Ensuring Access to Information

Information systems contain data that can tell the story of what is being done in the agency. This is a story of accountability and the information produced can be used to advocate for change. But there are another series of questions that need to be asked if the supervisory manager is to fully explore technological needs. How do team members learn about the latest research, the most recent advances in their areas of expertise? How are programs developed with an eye to the latest models, the best practice examples? How do employees keep up to date?

The days of trudging off to the library are numbered, and our experience indicates that few managers or team members in many agencies have time to do that anyway. It is rather academic to think that grants are written, programs designed, and problems solved with all the latest literature at one's fingertips, much less read and digested. If it is important for the agency to have access to the latest information and to be able to find research results and program models quickly, then the technological means are available via the Internet.

The best known features and applications of the Internet include E-mail, file transfer protocol (FTP), Gopher, and the World Wide Web (WWW). Determining which Internet provider is appropriate for your organization involves answering some basic questions: (1) Who will access the Internet—a person or an entire organization? (2) What will be done with that access—research, E-mail, or establishing a web site? (3) What plans does your organization have for future growth on the Internet? (Zeff, 1996, p. 29).

There are many implications to the answers to these questions. First, who will access the Internet has implications for what hardware is available. In other words, it might be preferred that everyone has access, but the cost of equipment is such that financial constraints limit the number who will. If everyone will have access or at least a large number of employees, then this will have an impact on the organization's culture.

Second, for those persons who do have access, training is a major consideration. Given the proliferation of workshops, short courses, training events, and other opportunities offered by community colleges, universities, computer stores, and others, there should be little trouble locating training resources. In fact, volunteers and other staff who are computer literate may be recruited to conduct training. The problem, of course, is time. It takes practice and time to fully use Internet resources. Supervisory managers need to be open to the fact that workers will need time to explore access to the Internet and what that means.

Third, there is the need to recognize Internet User Policies in the organization. Zeff (1996) points out that most organizations have unofficial protocols in place about the use of office equipment for personal, as opposed to professional, business. For example, there is typically an understanding about personal phone calls at work and the use of the copy machine for personal items. The reason the supervisory manager may need to consider drawing on these same protocols stems from the high entertainment value of the Internet, as well as the ease in sending personal as well as work- related messages via E-mail. The same protocols will likely suffice, but it may be necessary to discuss these protocols in view of the new technology in place. Indeed, these are the human consequences of technological shifts that must be considered by the supervisory manager.

Having asked what is needed and having determined what technology might meet those needs, the next task is to nurture staff through the inevitable transitions that need to occur to fully realize the new technological possibilities. Because human service professionals are often people-oriented people, they may not have gone into this work to become totally computer proficient. However, with the rapid changes in technology that have occurred, it will be the rare organization that will not seize opportunities to use technological advances to their advantage. We now turn to the implications of using various technologies for agency practice.

IMPLICATIONS OF TECHNOLOGICAL ADVANCES FOR AGENCY PRACTICE

Zeff (1996) cites three reasons why an organization should go online. "First, is the fact that the Internet enhances an organization's ability to communicate with its members, its staff, and the general public. Second, the Internet provides incredible access to information around the world. Third, the Internet is an exciting new fundraising medium" (1996, p. 33). Each of these reasons is important for supervisory managers to understand since each influences the way in which technology can be viewed as a vehicle for enhanced agency practice. Not only do individual employees have to recognize the implications of technologies for their work with consumers, but they will need to join in a vision of what these changes mean for the entire organization. Supervisory managers will be the conveyers of this connection between employee and agency.

Zeff (1996) points out that the Internet can increase internal and external communication among various employees and selected constituencies exponentially. Being on-line means that an organization is accessible 24 hours a day, 365 days a year if someone is interested in having information about that agency. Moreover, anyone in the world can gain access to agency information by means of a few keystrokes. This revolutionizes an agency's ability to market itself, to get information out, and to project a desired public image.

E-mail allows employees to access messages at any time of the day or night from any location that has the appropriate equipment. Responding to E-mail messages is quick, and copying messages and replies to other parties becomes routine. The ability to attach and send entire files in E-mail messages allows others to receive information quickly and to revise documents on the screen and send them back to the originator.

E-mail mailing lists also allow staff to read the latest happenings from colleagues with similar interests. There are two types of mailing lists—a read-only server and a discussion group. Read-only servers are controlled by their owners and information is posted for anyone who accesses the list to read. On the other hand, discussion groups are literally mailing lists of persons who choose to interact around topics of interest. The software that operates such a list is called a list server.

The value of mailing lists in gathering information is as follows: 1) allows access to a group of potential experts, 2) allows timely answers to questions, 3) facilitates networking, and 4) assists in developing a research strategy or finding related information. (Zeff, 1996, pp. 49–50)

An example of a very active list server is the one sponsored by the Association for Research on Nonprofit Organizations and Voluntary Action (ARNOVA). Members of this list from all over the world interact on a regular basis over such concerns as the accountability of nonprofit organizations, strategic planning, and the use of volunteers.

As an agency moves toward having an on-line presence, the entire culture of communication and information sharing changes. Developing a web site allows agencies to provide information to others in a way they could not have afforded to do before. Polished brochures and expensive mailing costs are no longer the primary medium for exchanging information, as hundreds (perhaps thousands) of persons are able to access the agency's web site.

In consulting with nonprofit agencies, Zeff (1996) points out how these organizations learned about others doing similar work and even established connections with sister agencies around the country, once they were on-line and running. This points to the potential for advocating for change by forming electronic alliances with others. More and more agencies are relying on E-mail communications through list servers that contain hundreds of members. Getting the word out to everyone on a mailing list used to be an incredibly time-consuming task. Setting up telephone trees used to be another method of spreading the word. Now it is possible to follow legislative change day by day via E-mail, contact an entire alliance when a particular bill is to be heard, and maintain communication on an hourly basis should that be necessary. The potential to engage in outreach and advocacy are incredible.

The agency's ability to gather information is expanded beyond imagination with Internet access. Once on-line that organization can literally communicate with anyone in the world that is also on-line, accessing research and technical information in an incredibly rapid fashion. Searchable databases, directories, bibliographies, dictionaries, and resource lists provide everything from access to the Library of Congress to the local university's holdings. All of the student grant applications, program plans, responses to a consumer's inquiry, and access to the latest research is available to agency staff. This has implications for continuing education and keeping staff up to date as they have opportunities to locate information on the leading edge without leaving their desks.

Fundraising is another aspect of going on-line that is critical to agency survival. Reaching large numbers of people quickly can happen by going on-line. This will require excellent marketing and communication skills in packaging what goes out. Whether soliciting directly or asking for persons who visit the agency's web site to contribute, agency managers will want to come up with creative ways to spread the word about the work of the organization. In addition, as more and more sources of funding create their own web sites, agencies looking for monies can obtain the latest guidelines and lists of grantees from these organizations as well. In a way, the potential for how the agency positions itself and how much information is accessed is limitless.

SO WHY ARE THERE STILL PROBLEMS?

The excitement about opening the agency to a larger world arena must be tempered by the realities that accompany technological change. We have painted a bright picture of the incredible potential open to managerial supervisors, their staff, and agency administrators as they encounter the world of possibilities. However, choices must be made that involve a great deal of resources, including expensive financial commitments on the front end in buying the necessary hardware and software. These are not easy decisions and we have all heard stories of the agency that invested in the hardware and software that would put them on the map, only to find that they had so many unanticipated problems that they could not even use what they had purchased. A miscalculation such as that could bankrupt an organization.

Therefore, not surprisingly, the first problem with the new technologies is that they are costly. Not only is it costly to be sure everyone has the equipment that they need, but there must be someone responsible for maintaining that equipment. This person must have not only the technical skill to diagnose problems and respond accordingly, but also reasonable interpersonal skills to interact with distraught staff members who are fearful that they have just lost valuable documents. Factoring in the costs of on-going technical support, as well as recognizing the necessity for upgrading both hardware and software, means that continuing resources will have to be devoted to the agency's commitment to remain an active and viable part of the technological world. For example, one agency established a computer advisory committee that surveyed staff to determine their needs. Based on the re-sponses received, the committee formulated a priority plan and took it back to agency staff for their consideration. Fine-tuning this plan created a dialogue among the committee members and interested others, and helped everyone feel a part of the decision-making process about what equipment would be ordered next and who would receive it.

Once a unit has what is needed, staff who are not computer lit-erate or who need to upgrade their computer skills must be pro-vided with training opportunities. As mentioned earlier, there are many places to go to get short courses or minisessions on specific software programs. Technical assistance may be available from various vendors as well, particularly when something happens that no one can seemingly explain. A quick phone call to the vendor's helpline may save hours of time trying to resolve a problem. How-ever, what the managerial supervisor must consider is that if staff members are to become computer proficient, they will need time to practice their new skills.

One supervisor recently told us about how frustrated he was with staff learning to play solitaire on agency time. Seeing this as highly inap-propriate, he admonished them. Later he recognized that the skills learned in playing this game were actually skills these same staff mem-bers needed to fully explore and use their new equipment. Mouse proficiency, for example, was learned easily in a game of solitaire and would carry over to all other operations. Ironically, he was heard telling a recent new employee to practice her skills by playing a round of solitaire every so often.

Getting up to speed may mean some initial "down time," but this is necessary if staff members are going to fully use the equipment they have.

Legal issues surrounding the use of the Internet are still being formulated as persons in power come to grips with exactly what this explosion of connection is all about. Until that time, it is important to recognize that technological fundraising and lobbying are still ruled by those same laws that normally cover these activities. For example, if a United Way Agency is not allowed to solicit monies on their own during a United Way Campaign Drive, then the agency may want to consult with United Way officials about what this means for their ongoing fundraising strategy over the Internet. Comprehensive sources that discuss the nuts and bolts of fundraising are available (Perlman & Bush, 1996) and should be consulted just as they would be for any type of solicitation. Similarly, lobbying is an activity governed by law. If, for example, a nonprofit agency decides to spend more than 10% of its time organizing members of an electronic mailing list to lobby state legislators for a particular set of bills, then this could be very problematic. Confidentiality is also extremely important. In previous chapters we reinforced that E-mail is not totally private. Staff members need to be very careful about how they use electronic forms of communication when discussing anything of a confidential nature. Blocking access to certain data on the MIS will be essential for managerial supervisors in health and human service agencies.

There are a number of legal issues inherent in using the Internet as well. Questions surrounding who has jurisdiction over cyberspace, the right to freedom of expression, who owns materials transmitted electronically, rights to privacy, safety, and equal access (Zeff, 1996) are being asked more and more. These issues are ones with which the supervisory manager will want to be familiar.

CONCLUSION

We began this chapter with a reminder that the term *technology* has a broad-based meaning encompassing both hardware (computers, monitors, printers, faxes, telephones, etc.) and software (Windows, Excel, Word, Internet Explorer, etc.). But we also referred to technology as those procedures that actually become part of agency practice—the ways in which people do the skilled work of helping people to transform their lives. The managerial supervisor's role is to use the more concrete technologies discussed above to support those service or client-focused technologies used by the professionals on their teams.

Given the importance of understanding technology, it is necessary to identify issues that emerge when considering organizational technology. Of critical importance is recognizing that managerial supervisors must be aware of and willing to learn current technology while still continuing to do the daily tasks necessary to perform their jobs. They will have to set limits so that they can become updated in an efficient manner.

Hasenfeld (1983) identifies other issues that should be considered. First, there are inevitable disagreements over what the hoped-for outcome will be. In a rehabilitation program, for example, is the desired goal to help a person become independent or to develop an accommodating environment to meet that person's need? The first approach may use the technology of physical therapy to get a person to walk again, whereas an accommodating environment may require the full range of assistive devices that will equip a person to negotiate his or her environment. Determining what technology to use could conceivably be determined by contacting experts in the field in order to locate the latest research on this type of rehabilitation. Second, there is the difficulty involved in selecting a reasonable intervention. Is a behavioral approach more logical for a client than a more psychoanalytical approach? Again, continuing one's professional development in a time of rapid change may mean that the worker debating this approach will need access to a list server of persons who do these types of interventions.

Third, how can clients be matched appropriately with interventions when assessment criteria are often uncertain and ambiguous? For example, if a mini-mental status test indicates that a person has only occasional lucid intervals, is it possible to determine if assessment questions are being answered reliably? Perhaps, a human service worker who wants to determine what the developer of the test would do when faced with this dilemma can actually E-mail that person and ask this question directly. Fourth, quality control is almost impossible since there is so much dependence on the relationship established between workers and clients. What, then, is successful? Hasenfeld (1983) contends that because the raw materials of human service organizations are people, human service technologies are "moral" technologies. There is incredible discretion used on the part of professionals in terms of what technologies will be used.

The point is that human service agencies have been using diverse and complicated technologies for years. Supervisory managers are constantly working with staff to update their technological skills in how they intervene with consumers—whether through the latest advances in assessment, care planning, counseling, resource mobilization, quality assurance, outcome measurement, and a host of other areas. These approaches are humanized already, given the fact that they require workers to have intense interpersonal relationships with clients, and these human service technologies are the foundation on which interventions are customized to meet consumer needs. In addition, the supervisory manager must now figure out creative ways to support these same workers in having the latest information at their fingertips through the Internet, and support the most efficient ways possible to record assessment, reassessment, and intervention data. Perhaps laptop computers will be used. Perhaps data entry persons, who can be sure that this information becomes part of the agency's database, are needed. But these technologies must be appreciated as a means to an end—they facilitate the ability of the human service worker to use and update their skills. Whatever technological decisions are made by managers, these decisions must be thoughtful and relevant both in terms of staff needs and agency requirements.

PART TWO
ORGANIZATIONAL ADAPTIVE STRATEGIES

IN Part 2 we discuss those strategies that can be used by managerial supervisors in dealing with issues that are part of the daily activities of professionals who supervise others.

Chapter 5, "Facilitating Communication," focuses on the importance of language, both verbal and written. Since misunderstandings are commonplace, the savvy supervisor anticipates how to provide alternative ways of getting one's message across to others. In Chapter 6 we examine the increasingly important need to value and fully address the needs of a diverse workforce. In "Supporting Diversity," we explore how managerial supervisors will need skills not only to recognize and celebrate differences, but also to establish new norms in the workplace so that creative work can be done. "Creating and Sustaining Interdisciplinary Teams," the topic of Chapter 7, stresses the importance of learning how to supervise persons not only from one's own professional field but also from other professions as well.

Communication, supporting diversity, and creating interdisciplinary teams all lead to a discussion of "Motivating, Appraising, and Rewarding" employees, the subject of Chapter 8. In a time of uncertainty in human service organizations, it is critcally important to motivate staff through performance evaluation and reward systems. Chapter 9 concerns "Protecting Managers as Workers." Managerial supervisors must learn to take care of themselves just as they respect and care for the persons whom they supervise. And last, Chapter 10 provides an overview of "Evaluating Program Effectiveness" with a systematic approach to program evaluation that takes into account the complexity inherent in this process.

5

Facilitating Communication

Effective communication is a constant challenge in all aspects of human life—home, work, and play. The challenge is amplified as expectations increase for information to be disseminated faster and to more people. This challenge is faced by managerial supervisors in human service organizations today. Agencies are continually being transformed. They are modifying programs and services to keep pace with new consumer needs; they are participating in multiparty alliances and employing teams to work more inclusively and productively. At the same time, consumers and staffs are becoming more diverse, adding yet another layer of complexity to the human service workplace.

Just as the changing workforce raises the possibility of recognizing and mobilizing incredible strengths from diversity and reform, it also reinforces the need for effective communication skills by supervisory managers. This presents supervisors with yet another paradox: *as new technology facilitates the potential for diminished face-to-face interaction, the importance of interpersonal communication is increasingly recognized.*

In previous chapters we reinforced the concepts of organizational and professional cultures as a key to understanding human service organizations. These are equally important in facilitating communication within organizations. Schein (1992) identifies the basic components needed to literally form and fully integrate an organizational culture. The very first component is "creating a language and conceptual categories," and he indicates that "if members can not communicate with and understand each other, a group is impossible by definition" (p. 70). Having a common language makes it possible for consensus to occur and allows group members to exchange both verbal and nonverbal behaviors that lead to full communication.

To any managerial supervisor, Schein speaks the obvious. In fact, the importance of communication is likely one of the only things on which all management theorists and practitioners would agree—of course, communication is key! Tom Peters (1987), the popular management guru of the excellence movement, proclaimed that "communication is everyone's panacea for everything" (p. 263). He goes on to explain that no matter how well designed computer information systems are, if organizational, people, and attitudinal issues are not fully considered, communication breakdown is inevitable. The same is true for all information-dissemination systems. Communication in the workplace is not simply about words; it integrates values, experiences, and behaviors into a process that to be effective must produce a shared comprehension and ground joint action.

In this chapter, we provide direction for how managerial supervisors may better understand communication and what strategies can be used to enhance this critical aspect of organizational culture. We begin with a brief overview of the importance of communication, then focus more specifically on understanding and skill building.

THE SIGNIFICANCE OF COMMUNICATION

Few people in either the theoretical or the applied management literature argue about whether communication is important.

However, issues arise over *how* people go about making communication happen. The ability to truly communicate well is considered an art form in management.

We suggest that communication is increasingly important today because there is more potential for misunderstanding among diverse workforce members, professions, and organizations. Also, organizations are often large, providing less opportunity for face-to-face interaction. As teams are formed within the workplace and alliances are developed across organizations, the potential for miscommunication expands exponentially. This increases the responsibility for managers, as they must continuousy attend to the interdependence of context and culture.

Hammer (1996) presents a view of the contemporary organization that is highly focused on process. His basic argument is that the Industrial Revolution turned its back on process by breaking everything down into specific tasks. By having people assigned to specialized tasks, each person became somewhat of an expert in one area but had little knowledge and therefore no ownership of the full process. Technically, each person could do his or her tasks by the book, but the program could actually fail because no one was looking out for the whole. Fabricant (1985) similarly argued that social workers no longer saw the whole as they did when they worked with the process from beginning to end; instead their work has also become partialized.

The essence of both authors' argument is that understanding the overall process and its goals is critical to achieving what one wants to do. Therefore, the people who are part of the process need to understand it in its entirety, and they need to see how their work fits with the work of others in achieving the deisired ends.

> It is the process owner's responsibility to provide the team with the knowledge of the process so that they can perform it. The process owner "owns" not the performance of the process but its design, sharing it with all the teams who perform it. Thus the process owner has responsibility for the design of the process and its documentation, and for training process performers in its structure and conduct. (Hammer, 1996, p. 77)

The managerial supervisor becomes the "process owner," responsible for full communication with team members. This is quite a responsibility, but it is the challenge faced by competent managerial supervisors in the contemporary human service organization.

One way to begin infusing communication throughout the organization is to intentionally build it into the culture. A culture that promotes communication is one in which it is assumed that misunderstanding is normal, that it is acceptable to ask for clarification, that redundancy in communication is needed, and that people are not mind readers. These assumptions are very different from the traditional power and control concerns many persons have in the workplace, as they attempt to maintain a sense of professional integrity by not asking too many questions and appear to know what they are supposed to do.

The paradox in communication, therefore, is all around us. Although we have the opportunity to communicate via machine and have limited time to interact face to face, we cannot afford to avoid making time for interaction. Given these pressures, what can a managerial supervisor do to address these concerns that permeate the workplace?

ASSESSING METHODS OF COMMUNICATION

Misunderstandings are all too common in communication attempts. The way people use language, written and verbal, is critical to communication, and the managerial supervisor needs to have skills in making language work. If language is indeed the glue that holds communications together and helps to define the organizational culture, then managers must possess skills in understanding what language means to people and be able to model the appropriate use of language.

A first step in strengthening the communication process is for the managerial supervisor to assess the methods that are being used to communicate in the workplace. Does the organization use in-person communication, telephone, voicemail, written communications, and electronic mail? Since effective communication depends on the degree to which the communicator can match the mode with the context and people with whom he or she is communicating (Dreher, 1996), we will briefly examine each.

IN-PERSON COMMUNICATION

In-person communication is formal and informal, verbal and non-verbal. Formal communication occurs in meetings and likely conforms to prearranged schedules. For example, teams may meet on Wednesday mornings, a task force may meet once a month, and full staff may meet once a quarter. These exchanges may be contentious or pleasant, depending on the dynamics of the group, the stage of their development, and the issues presented. These interchanges may be dominated by subgroups or extroverted individuals in the organization and will be the place in which body language and gestures are interpreted differently by each person in attendance. One cannot assume in these formal meetings that everyone hears the same thing and usually when minutes of the meeting are circulated, there will be some disagreement about "what was really said." Yet, these formal exchanges are part of the organizational culture, and how meetings are viewed are important to the managerial supervisor's understanding of how the culture operates.

In-person exchanges are not always formal. The interactions among staff in the hallways or as they work on team projects are ongoing, and these communications also are critical to the operation of the agency. The physical proximity of staff, colocation of team members, the way in which the office is set up, who has a window, who has privacy, how easy it is for clients to access an office, and a host of other factors form the context in which informal interpersonal interaction occurs.

If people are in the field more than they are in the office, personal interaction may be somewhat limited, and adjustments may have to be made so that communication does not falter. If staff members come to the office only 2 days a week, additional efforts to keep them connected to the team are likely to be necessary. Similarly, as individuals become more proficient electronically, virtual offices in which people operate from home diminish the potential for face-to-face communication on a regular basis. The managerial supervisor needs to be aware of the implications of these changes in structure on daily work.

Nonverbal communication is another important aspect of personal interactions and must be considered in both informal and formal exchanges. Haynes (1989, pp. 65–66) indicates that there are gender differences in how people make eye contact and for how long, in how people posture, in the use of space, in touching and its appropriateness, and even in how much people smile. Similar differences in style can be found in various cultures and subcultures, even though all are verbally speaking the same language. Given potential differences, misinterpretations in what is intended can occur. The managerial supervisor needs to be sensitive to differences in nonverbal communication that staff bring to the workplace and continually look to clarify actions that are perceived to be problematic.

TELEPHONE AND VOICEMAIL

Today's workplace is still very tied to telephone communications, but the nature of that communication has altered radically. It is becoming more rare to access persons directly. Large agencies often meet the public via interactive voicemail systems in which clients and others are required to listen to lists of instructions and select the numbered options that will direct them to their desired source of information. Depending on the individual, this can be a tremendous barrier or an easy way to quickly reach the appropriate party. In human service organizations in which clients are often under stress, the supervisory manager will want to consider just how user friendly these devices are.

For example, in a large multipurpose human service organization there was an automated voicemail system. Everyone who called had to listen to a series of instructions and a listing of names. Direct access to individuals on this system was not possible. Several staff members were confronted by irate clients who said that they were inaccessible, and the staff members agreed. The managerial supervisor listened to the staff's concerns. Together they agreed that each staff member could decide to use a personal answering machine or the voicemail system. The supervisory manager helped staff negotiate the issue, and staff members were able to choose the alternative they preferred—being available to clients by phone or protected from client interruptions—rather than being constrained by one standardized approach.

Written Communication

Human service organizations have always been dependent on written communications, and that will remain. Yet, the format of these communications is changing as alternative methods arise. Written communication has even greater potential to be misunderstood because it is disembodied. Intonation is missing, and readers may have different interpretations of what has been written. The following situation involving a small nonprofit human service agency serving older persons illustrates this point.

The managerial supervisor wanted to set up a task force of persons to name an employee of the year. This was a controversial decision because staff had mixed feelings about the use of such human relations tactics, with some staff seeing the naming of an employee as competitive and manipulative and others seeing it as a chance for recognition of hard work done. No one wanted to be on the task force because it would inevitably mean that some staff felt unrecognized for their efforts. Consequently, the supervisory manager wrote a memo to four persons that began with these words: "I invite you to participate on an ad hoc task force to name the employee of the year."

Each recipient read this statement differently. One person assumed it meant that he had the option not to accept the invitation, and he threw the memo away. Another person assumed she needed to RSVP to the word "invitation," and she wrote an E-mail message declining the invitation. The third person assumed that he was assigned to the task force by his supervisor and that this was a command performance, so he waited to hear when the meeting would be set. The fourth person went to the supervisor to clarify what an "invitation" to a task force meant. The managerial supervisor thought she was making their appointment to the task force more palatable by phrasing it as an invitation, but her use of language was virtually meaningless, and no one felt good about the memo.

Electronic Mail (E-mail)

E-mail is one form of written communication that requires special attention, in part because of the dramatic rate at which its use is increasing, but also because of the technological issues associated with it, which were discussed in Chapter 4 on humanizing technology. Managerial supervisors not only need to understand how to use their own E-mail systems, but they also need to examine the overall effectiveness of their organizational E-mail systems. In Chapter 2 we discussed the legal implications of E-mail and the fact that this type of communication is not entirely private. This is important to keep in mind, since staff often send personal as well as professional messages via E-mail.

E-mail is a unique communication technique because it is interactive, but, as with other forms of written communication, eliminates the use of intonation and body language to promote understanding. In that regard, it is more informal than many written communications such as memos, but more formal than in-person and telephone communications.

An example of one organization's attempt to move to E-mail communications between task force meetings presents some of the salient issues managers need to consider when using this form of communication.

> The supervisory manager decided to work through issues between face-to-face meetings by posing them on E-mail and letting staff send their responses and thoughts as they came to mind. This seemed to be working well. There was a lot of communication back and forth as people responded to issues and mulled over what to do.
>
> However, no ground rules had been established, and soon people were complaining about how fellow task force members were using the system. Some tended to monopolize the dialogue. One resorted to "flaming" others over E-mail with emotionally charged and inappropriate remarks when something did not sit well. The use of all capital letters by one person made others think she was shouting at them, and there was a lack of structure in following the dialogue since people contributed at will and messages were not received in any certain order.
>
> Ironically, there were also members of the task force who seemed to be much more agreeable and subject to consensus over E-mail be-

cause they enjoyed the isolation of composing their responses at their convenience and actually did not enjoy the interaction of face-to-face task meetings. In the next meeting, the managerial supervisor asked that the group establish protocols for how to use E-mail for communicating. Having established their E-mail etiquette and learning more about how the members approached communication, the manager was also better able to balance the use of E-mail and face-to-face relationships within the task force.

The electronic mail message of today may be replacing the written interoffice memo of yesterday. By sending a batchmail message to all staff or E-mailing members of a LISTSERV, an idea, a change in a meeting date, a new program, or anything else can be announced quickly and easily. This poses another challenge for the managerial supervisor who will have to consider the implications of what needs to be in written form and distributed and what can suffice with an electronic message.

For example, in organizations in which the technology is not always reliable or not available to all staff, people can actually be dropped from the information dissemination system if they cannot access their mail electronically. Consequently, use of written announcements to back up what was said electronically may be an important way to reinforce the communication as well as to ensure that everyone gets the message.

UNDERSTANDING AND USING LANGUAGE

There are a number of things the supervisory manager can do to understand and use language well. These include recognizing communication context, identifying metaphors and symbols, and acknowledging different communication modes and styles.

RECOGNIZING THE COMMUNICATION CONTEXT

Heyman (1994) indicates that we must assume misunderstanding is normal. He points out that all words have multiple meanings but "these meanings are narrowed down by the context in which the words are used. . . . Until we have a context for their meaning, all words and combinations of words, such as phrases and sentences, are ambiguous" (p. 9). Managerial supervisors have to recognize the context in which they are making a statement, but the listener may actually establish his or her own context, which changes the meaning of what is heard. We cannot make assumptions that language will be understood: the most carefully designed memo, the most clever E-mail message, and the most engaging interpersonal conversation can go awry because of misunderstanding.

IDENTIFYING METAPHORS AND SYMBOLS

A metaphor is "understanding and experiencing one kind of thing in terms of another" (Lakoff & Johnson, 1980, p. 5). Gareth Morgan's (1997) compelling analysis of the images we use to describe organizations is based on metaphorical thinking. He contends that the effective managerial supervisor who recognizes that metaphors are constantly being used to communicate images of organizations. The beauty of metaphor is that it serves to clarify things that are subtle and difficult to understand. Yet, metaphors are value laden. They may imply things to people that are not intended. The paradox of the metaphor is that it scripts one into thinking in a particular way, possibly focusing on one image to the exclusion of others as it sets a frame for viewing the situation. For example, the managerial supervisor who compares the agency to a well-oiled machine projects a mechanical metaphor; the person who describes the organization as an organism in a turbulent environment presents a very different metaphor.

The images used to describe the work will be heard differently by various listeners. Recognizing the metaphorical nature of language, and being flexible in how metaphors are used, is an art that must be developed by the effective manager. "Skilled leaders and managers develop the knack of reading situations with various scenarios in mind and of forging actions that seem appropriate to the understandings thus obtained" (Morgan, 1997, p. 3). The managerial supervisor must focus wholly on what is occurring in the present with an awareness so intense she or he is "aware of what is going on within and without" (Nhat Hanh, 1995, p. 204).

Acknowledging Communication Styles and Modes

Supervisors and staff members have individual styles and preferences for one or more modes of communicating. Some are more flamboyant than others. Some work in harmony, and others clash. To effectively facilitate communication, the supervisory manager must begin by recognizing her or his own style for

> working, communicating and learning/teaching. . . . Perhaps the most important thing is to be aware of your own style and repertoire, the latter meaning the degree of flexibility and range you can offer when working with different people with different needs in different contexts. (Brown & Bourne, 1996, p. 23)

Only then can a manager begin to understand others' styles.

Interesting work on communication style has been conducted by sociolinguists. Deborah Tannen (1994) indicates that each "individual has a unique style, influenced by a personal history of many influences such as geographic region, ethnicity, class, sexual orientation, occupation, religion and age—as well as unique personality and spirit" (p. 13). She focuses on gender, but readily recognizes that gender is only one of multiple factors that affect communication.

Tannen (1990, p. 42) introduces the concept of "genderlects" as a form of cross-cultural communication, communication that literally comes from two different cultural perspectives—female and male. She contends that understanding these differences is critical if we are to avoid placing blame and treating women inequitably. She contends that women tend toward emphasizing connection and establishing rapport, whereas men tend toward reporting information. In a workplace situation this may mean that a female employee reaches out to establish a relationship, whereas a male colleague might see this as inappropriate and even unproductive behavior on the job.

Given the predisposition to seek rapport, the following situation was confusing to a female member in a human service agency. She had located new data on the subject of child abuse that she wanted to share with a colleague on her team. Excited about finding this new information, she came into his office and said, "I've found something else for the report!" He looked it over carefully and replied, "Yes, this is good. You win, we'll include it." Perplexed, she asked, "Win what?" "Well, you win, we'll include it," he repeated. She walked down the hall without understanding. He had framed the conversation as a win–lose: she had located information he had not found. She had seen it as a win–win: they could both benefit from it. Similar conversations occur in the hallways of agencies every day, and they reflect profound differences in conversational style that need to be addressed in order to optimize communication and understanding.

Tannen (1990) also contends that women and men approach problems differently and that this can get in the way of clear communication. Women often present a problem with the intent to gain confirmation and solicit a discussion of the issues. Men tend to think that their colleagues are asking them to help problem solve and may feel compelled to try to solve the difficulty. This puts stress on the relationship since the male colleague may see the female's request as a demand for him to solve what she really just needs to talk through. Tannen's work is instructive in illustrating the possible nature of miscommunications between men and women, given the different ways in which they are socialized.

Similarly, Cox (1994) tells us that culturally diverse groups experience more potential for miscommunication than homogeneous groups. He contends that "greater patience and acceptance of different standards of oral communication efficiency may pay dividends in the quality of problem solving and innovation" (p. 125), but what it requires is a workforce that is culturally sensitive. For example, his research reveals that Asian-Americans may find the workplace communication styles of Anglo-Americans and African-Americans rude and inhibiting. It is also our experience that the use of direct language by some ethnic groups can be uncomfortable for people whose culture is less direct in its verbal communications.

Beyond gender and cultural differences, the predilection for differing modes of communication also affects the efficacy of interactions. Communication modes, which can include visual (i.e., seeing), auditory (i.e., hearing/talking), and kinaesthetic (i.e., feeling), are established in childhood and are brought to the workplace after years of use (Brown & Bourne, 1996). However, the behaviors associated with these modes may not always be helpful in communicating.

> For example, in a recent board meeting, a staff person was presenting a report on a program with which she was very familiar. As was her style, the staff member used her hands a great deal in the presentation. One board member commented to her afterward that it was nice of her to sign the entire presentation. He remarked, "I had so much interest in watching you sign, that I forgot to listen." Obviously, communication was hampered and the message lost because of her reliance on her hands.

Variation in orientation toward work as well as approaches to learning and teaching further impact communication. Managerial supervisors may find that employees who are more outcome or task oriented can be frustrated by colleagues who are highly process oriented. Similarly, persons learn differently (i.e., orally, visually, etc.), and since supervision is tied to encouraging professional development and growth, the ability to communicate new information in relation to the supervisee's work style is critical.

Four learning styles, accommodator, assimilator, diverger, and converger, have been identified (Smith & Kolb, 1986, pp. 13–14). These styles are based on two continua—(1) concrete to abstract and (2) active to reflective, as presented in Table 5.1.

Table 5.1: Four Learning Styles

	Concrete	Abstract
Active	Accommodator	Diverger
Reflective	Converger	Assimilator

The accommodator stresses concrete experience and active experimentation. For example, an employee with this learning style who needed to learn a new computer program would want to sit at the computer and be actively engaged in trying the procedure. To maximize learning, the approach would be very concrete and interactive. The accommodator would not spend time reflecting about the importance of the computer program or trying to figure out the abstract nuances that led to its software development.

The assimilator, on the other hand, would learn in a manner almost opposite to the accomodator, being much more abstract and reflective. This employee would want to understand how a computer works and the conceptualization behind the software program being used. The assimilator would also want to reflect about the implications of using this program, seeing the context in which the program would be used, and how that would impact work.

The converger's learning style would require concrete hands-on experience, much like the accomodator, but would reflect on this experience, much like the assimilator. The converger would want to be at the computer to see what happens with the new program, but would be just as happy to watch someone else perform the operations.

Last, the diverger's learning style is both abstract and active—opposite the learning style of the converger. The diverger would want to understand how the computer works (much like the assimilator), but would want to be active in experimenting with the program.

These learning styles are impacted by numerous factors, including personality, education, culture, and professional environment.

Recognizing that people learn in these different ways emphasizes the importance of customizing training and education experiences so that information is fully received (Brown & Bourne, 1996). The Learning Style Inventory (LSI) is one tool to assist managerial supervisors in this task (Kolb, 1985) as it identifies individuals' styles.

STRATEGIES FOR EFFECTIVE COMMUNICATION

Since language is the primary way of communicating, and every word is symbolic, effective communication begins with recognizing the complexity of language. Yet, the supervisory manager must go beyond recognizing this complexity and figure out just how to

convey clear messages. How is this done? We believe that supervisory managers must confront conflict, learn to use strategic talk,
and clarify written materials if they are to be effective.

CONFRONTING CONFLICT

The managerial supervisor has a responsibility to create a climate
that is open to communication with his or her supervisees. Although it is hoped that the overall organizational culture will reinforce an open climate, established organizational norms may
serve more as communication barriers than conduits of information. One barrier frequently seen in the contemporary workplace
is a *we–they* mentality in which administrators are cast as "those
persons who do not understand us" against staff who feel misunderstood. Communication in these situations may break down to
the point that it is not possible and an impartial third party such
as a mediator may be called in to intervene between management
and line staff. This unfortunate situation indicates that communication has broken down to the point that all perspective is lost.

If it can be assumed that misunderstanding is a normal part of
communication, then it can be understood that communication
is something that everyone must continuously work to improve.
Instead of an administration that does not understand staff needs,
it can legitimately be said that no one truly understands another's
needs and that this is not a malevolent plot. Instead, it is normal
that conflict will arise and miscommunication will occur.

Heyman (1994) suggests that there are steps that can be taken
to build an organizational culture that enhances communication,
including opening lines of communication, placing the responsibility for remedying the problems within the appropriate person's operational area, building a culture of clear communication
based on an atmosphere of trust and understanding, and "recognizing that the overall communication structure of an organization is only as strong as the communication skills of each person within the organization" (pp. 120–124). Thus it is OK to ask
for clarification and repetition to enhance understanding.

Although many persons who work in human services are skilled
advocates who deal with conflict on a daily basis outside the organization, inside the agency "instead of dealing with tensions as

they occur, people tend to wait until there is an explosion and stored up conflicts threaten to blow the entire organization apart" (Heyman, 1994, p. 173). Lakey, Lakey, Napier, and Robinson (1995) offer some perspective on how to handle communication breakdown and conflict. First, they suggest acknowledging that conflict. Even advocates in human service organizations may want to maintain a sense of harmony as they deny the tensions in the organization. Bringing conflict into the open is essential. Second, they suggest that trust has to be built, a process that takes time and deliberate planning. Third, they suggest establishing ground rules about how people will operate within the unit or organization. For example, a ground rule established by a team for its own behavior could be that 30 minutes into the meeting, the team will stop to assess how people are feeling about their participation in the meeting. Another ground rule could be that new ideas will not be criticized so that people can put their thoughts forward without fear of repercussion.

Feedback is critically important to good communication and an effective means in conflict resolution. However, it must be timely: the longer the manager waits to give feedback, the less likely it is to be effective. Managerial supervisors must also be generous in giving positive feedback, which recognizes the supervisee's work.

Lakey et al. (1995) suggest that third party assistance should be solicited if communication is just not working. There are times in the workplace where a neutral third party mediator is needed to actually facilitate the communication process. Communication conflicts are based in very different factors such as style or ego, politics or strategy differences, philosophical disagreements, or a host of other possibilities. Managerial supervisors must be adept at knowing when third party intervention is needed.

STRATEGICALLY TALKING

Heyman (1994) suggests that we get beyond mind reading and work toward "strategic talk" (p. 24). Strategic talk includes the use of "formulations, questions and answers, paraphrasing, examples, and stories [so that] we can achieve shared understanding by making shared context explicit" (pp. 36–37).

A formulation is a useful technique that rephrases what the supervisor has said and serves to clarify and/or summarize the issue.

> For example, a managerial supervisor is talking with a team member about his project. The manager asks, "How's it going?" The team member responds, "Well, okay, but there's a lot of paperwork to do. We don't know which forms to fill out first." The manager responds, "Would you like help in deciding which forms to do first?" By asking this question, the manager provides a formulation—a description of what she heard her supervisee saying.

This is not only active listening, but communication is enhanced by the participants saying out loud what they interpret the meaning of the talk to be.

Equally important for strategic talk are questions and answers. If it is assumed that misunderstanding is a usual occurrence, it is logical to ask questions and seek answers to clarify the difference. The managerial supervisor can enhance communication by setting a climate in which people are comfortable in asking questions and expecting answers from their supervisors. Otherwise, time is wasted as supervisees wonder exactly what they should do while the manager thinks the assignment is perfectly clear—an example of a misunderstanding. The culture should help workers understand that asking questions is a sign of competence.

Another element of strategic talk is paraphrasing. We often use paraphrasing in conversation, but Heyman (1994) suggests that people need to be more intentional about this element of communication.

> For example, an employee related to a supervisor the story of a client who had difficulty the night before when she attempted to call a beeper number. The supervisor stated, "She had trouble getting your beeper to work?" The employee replied, "No, it was Janice's beeper." By paraphrasing what the supervisor had heard, she was able to obtain clarification when the employee explained that they were speaking about someone else's beeper.

We use examples and stories in our ordinary conversation all the time, but part of strategic talk is doing so with intention.

For example, a geriatric education unit in a local hospital was attempting to orient new employees. The managerial supervisor who was giving the orientation provided several examples of how patients access the system and receive services. One example was given about a woman who had been in and out of the cardiac unit over a period of months, and required rehabilitation services on discharge. The woman's granddaughter, a single parent with a full-time job, had to spend endless hours negotiating the hospital and rehabilitation systems—two independent and different networks. By relaying the elderly woman's story, the manager helped the new employees vividly see how complicated it was to access geriatric care in a fragmented system and also highlighted the role that the front-line workers could play in making the process more user friendly.

Giving case examples and telling stories are ways of communicating meaning that goes beyond the policies and procedures in manuals and handbooks.

CLARIFYING WRITTEN MATERIALS

As discussed above, much of what is communicated in organizations is done in writing, in memos, and more recently, by E-mail. The use of plain language and direct communication in written communications is important in the human services where often professional terminology is not universally understood. Heyman (1994) offers some guidelines that may be useful in developing written materials. First, he suggests the use of plain language. Since language is often ambiguous and can be misinterpreted, it is important to work toward clarity in all written information. Clarity means eliminating jargon and being as concise and to the point as possible. It is probably best to have others read over one's written work before finalizing it; clarity will be enhanced by others' perspectives on the impact of the words used.

Furthermore, when writing memos, reports, and correspondence it should be understood that greater explanation may be required since no matter how clear people think they are being or how much thought goes into the writing, someone will interpret the document differently than intended. It may be useful to follow a memo concerning an important agency policy with a time for questions to be asked; everyone can read the information and clarification can be given as needed.

In written communication with clients, it is essential that human service organizations have hot lines or numbers that clients can call to ask questions. Simply having a handout or an information line with recorded information about how to access a service, approach a problem, or even how to contact a provider will not always be enough to facilitate clients accessing the services they need. Interaction for clarification is appropriate and should be ensured.

The underlying theme for dealing with conflict, talking strategically, and clarifying written communication is that these are ongoing processes that require repetition and continual clarification. The need for interpersonal communication to both supplement and complement written communication cannot be overemphasized as a way to keep the channels of understanding open.

CONCLUSION

In this chapter we introduced a communication paradox faced by health and human services managers and supervisors in the twenty-first century: Just as new technology facilitates the potential for diminished face-to-face interaction, the importance of interpersonal communication is increasingly recognized.

The significance of communication through language is crucial in the workplace as it helps to create and transmit the culture of an organization. To facilitate this awareness, the managerial supervisor must first understand the various methods of communication used in the work setting and utilize them to encourage an open environment in which people are free to ask questions, seek clarification, and express disagreement since the potential for misunderstanding always exists. Normalizing these expectations is something the supervisory manager must do.

Since there is a wide variety in cultural meanings and expectations, managerial supervisors must be comfortable in learning to confront conflict, using talk in a strategic manner, and working toward clarity in written communications. These are ongoing processes that form the glue within an organization and are critical in establishing a viable organizational culture.

The topics of the chapters that follow all depend on the managerial supervisor's effectiveness in this arena.

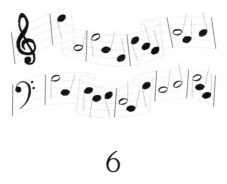

6

Supporting Diversity

The Neighborhood Health Center and Visiting Nurse Service was increasingly serving a diverse community as new Asian immigrants were joining African-American and Irish residents in the catchment area. The executive director, aware of the various cultural and ethnic needs of their consumers, aggressively sought to diversify the staff in order to reflect, as much as possible, the composition of the community. The executive was also sensitive to the fact that increasing diversity internally within the agency, and externally within the community, requires special attention in order to serve customers effectively, and also to help staff become a collegial group, comfortable with one another. The executive recognized that the situation would be well served by bringing in a consultant with expertise in the area.

This chapter seeks to support the managerial staff in human service organizations who similarly wish to address the reality of diversity within their agency. The focus on human service organizations merits special treatment since the mission of these organizations is concerned with meeting the needs of the wide array of consumers being served, with special attention to diversity. Differences of gender, ethnicity, social class, disability, age, race, and sexual orientation in both the staff and the consumers of the human services serve as a catalyst for recognizing the need for education in diversity for everyone in the organization. Since managerial supervisors are closer to the front-line professional providers of service, it is essential that they secure the knowledge and skills critical to shaping an already diverse workforce into high-performing human service organizations that can best meet the needs of equally diversified communities. Managerial supervisors must help their staff realize that when they choose a helping profession, part of the journey toward the organizational goal includes attention to diversity (Gallos, Ramsey, & Associates, 1997).

In this chapter we begin with a discussion of the changing population mix within the United States, followed by a definition of diversity. We then explore a four-level organizational typology of working with diversity, along with the costs and benefits inherent in the process. A parallel typology is then presented that shifts from the organizational to an individual perspective as a continuum of personal orientations toward diversity is discussed. We conclude with an example of diversity intervention in two human service settings that can serve to stimulate practical approaches to this challenge.

CHANGING CONTEXTS

Diversity, multiculturalism, intergroup dialogue, prejudice reduction, and pluralism are just a few of the terms used to describe the resurgence of community workshops, academic courses, and popular and scholarly articles that focus on facilitating the appreciation of differences among people. With its roots in the founding of this country (Thomas, 1998), this flurry of activity is not expected to diminish in the twenty-first century.

The oft quoted *Workforce 2000* report (Johnston & Packer, 1987) predicted that by the new millennium, although Caucasian men will continue to occupy 45% of our workplaces, they will represent only 15% of new workers. According to this forecast, 66% of new workers are expected to be women and 43% to be people of color, among whom 22% will be immigrants.

However, a more recent analysis of population trends (Fried-man & Ditomaso, 1996) dissents from this prediction of a dramatic increase in workforce diversity in the twenty-first century. These authors also take issue with other expectations regarding diversity as they argue (1) that gender diversity has now stabilized, (2) that the United States is not a magnet for skilled foreign workers, and (3) that greater diversity in the population of the United States will not ipso facto increase the economic opportunities for African-Americans. Whatever one's point of view, diversity remains a front burner issue in American society.

DEFINING DIVERSITY

A review of the literature reveals three theoretical orientations used to discuss diversity in the workforce: (1) the legal perspective, which focuses on organizational and individual knowledge of the law, (2) the anthropological perspective, which focuses on cultural and subcultural group awareness, and (3) the sociopsychological perspective, which focuses on similarities and differences among individual, group, and organizational values, knowledge, and skills (Muller & Parham 1998, p. 133). This chapter is grounded in sociopsychological theory, but we recognize the need for increasing our legal and anthropological awareness.

Although authors over the years have offered different definitions of the term "diversity" (Cox, 1993; Trickett, Watts, & Birman, 1993), Thomas (1996) presents a simple and direct definition, useful for managerial supervisors: "Diversity refers to any mixture of terms characterized by differences and similarities" (p. 5). The coupling of differences and similarities as necessary and sufficient components of the definition is a unique and critical contribution. Thomas gives the example of a jar of green jelly beans to which is added a cup of red jelly beans. The diversity is the mix of the two groups together, and diversity education must always address both groups in the mixture, attending to both their unique and common qualities. This definition has implications for all components of our organizations including policies and procedures, structure, marketing strategies, and systems of reward and promotion.

Accordingly, Thomas (1996) suggests the following proposi-
tions. First, diversity and organizational complexity (e.g., the way
roles and responsibilities are divided, and the number and type
of internal systems) are directly related in that as diversity increases so does complexity. Second, diversity is the totality of the
range of differences along the continuum of a specific organizational dimension: if the dimension under review is racial diversity, managerial supervisors could work with all the races throughout the organization or they could focus on one organizational
unit at a time (e.g., direct services or finance) to look for evidence
of a diversity mixture. Third, since diversity includes areas of difference and similarity, managerial supervisors must attend to both
areas concurrently.

It is precisely the need to deal with both the differences and
the similarities simultaneously that creates a paradox for the managerial supervisor. Since they seem to be contradictory requisites,
it is all the more challenging to acknowledge the validity of this
dual approach.

A way of managing this paradox is suggested by Gallos, Ramsey, and Associates (1997) who propose some nontraditional approaches that combine these two elements to generate a security
in self. This allows work with diversity to be seen "as an ongoing
challenge, an intellectual and interpersonal puzzle that all are in-
vited to solve. . . . Self pride and satisfaction come from the effort." Moreover, the developmental capacities of "tolerance for
ambiguity, acknowledgment of the social construction of knowledge, . . . appreciation of complexity as the norm" and recognizing that "despite differences there is an underlying unity in
human existence" (pp. 219–220) complete this listing of personal
and professional ingredients central to effectively managing the
paradox of uniqueness and similarity.

Reflecting on this paradox leads to the creation of the empathetic self, a visceral experience as well as a cognitive experience.
Empathetic leadership requires both recognition that self is different from another and an awareness of self in relation to another. The paradox of "uniqueness and similarity" requires risk
taking as empathic individuals must recognize that a sense of
wholeness requires being open to holding and including the

other as part of oneself. Consequently managerial supervisors must help staff develop a tolerance for ambiguity and complexity that includes the construct of diversity as the union of difference and sameness.

AN ORGANIZATIONAL TYPOLOGY
FOR SUPPORTING DIVERSITY

Organizations respect and endorse diversity to varying degrees. Consequently, classifying organizations based on their behaviors is a useful way for managerial supervisors to determine the level of effort required within their agencies to facilitate the full appreciation of differences and similarities. This is particularly relevent for human service organizations as it directly relates to their organizational mission.

A four-level typology of diversity involvement in organizations, useful for this discussion, has been suggested by The Equity Institute (1990).

Level 1 is the token *equal employment opportunity (EEO) organization* in which people of color and women are hired in accordance with EEO legislation, yet they have little or no real power and authority. Some of them may be in middle management positions, but these "tokens" of difference must walk and talk in strict concurrence with the agency's status quo to remain successful.

Level 2 is the *affirmative action organization* that recruits and hires people of color and women, and prohibits racist and sexist language and behavior. However, the password necessary for the select few to gain membership into positions of any authority is assimilation; the rest of these newcomers, especially those who attempt to deviate from the prevailing norm, quickly encounter what has been euphemistically referred to as the glass or, in the case of women of color, the lucite ceiling.

Level 3, the *self-renewing organization,* diligently and systematically assesses its culture, which Schein (1985) defines as those espoused and enacted values, behaviors, and symbols that comprise the essence of the organization. It uses the findings from its self-evaluation to design strategies that enhance individual and organizational satisfaction and productivity. This type of organization, which actively searches for ways to uncover and incorporate all the different perspectives in the organization into its culture, can be considered a culturally competent organization (Cross, 1988).

Level 4 describes the *pluralistic or multicultural organization.* Organizations at this level best embody the definition of pluralism offered by Brown University (1986):

> a state of affairs in which several distinct ethnic, religious and racial communities live side by side, willing to affirm each other's dignity, ready to benefit from each other's experience, and quick to acknowledge each other's contributions to the common welfare. (p. 9)

This organization supports a culture of true diversity or pluralism through its hiring and promotion practices as it prohibits all forms of discrimination, it sets new norms for social behavior within the institution, and also proactively seeks alliances with organizations of similar values and behaviors.

Many contemporary organizations are at Level 2, attempting to move toward Level 3. Although there has clearly been some positive change in organizational behavior in the twentieth century, this progression has included too few people, too few organizational dimensions, and has moved too slowly in striving to achieve a comfort level with their diversity (Thomas & Wetlaufer, 1997). Moving toward a Level 3 or Level 4 organization can take many paths.

Once the organizational level has been understood, a commitment from the executive level is essential for dealing with the organization's diversity; it then requires the involvement of all staff members. Managerial supervisors must realize that diversity is not embodied within any individual or group of individuals— it is socially constructed and collectively enacted. Consequently it must be collectively addressed.

AN ACTION MODEL FOR SUPPORTING DIVERSITY

There have been numerous and varied approaches used by organizations to deal with diversity, largely guided by two perspectives: "the *discrimination-and-fairness paradigm* and the *access-and-*

legitimacy paradigm" (Gummer, 1998, p. 92, emphasis in original). The former approach focuses on mentoring and career development while the latter approach focuses on "matching the demographics of the organization to those of critical consumer or constituent groups" (Gummer, 1998, p. 96). Although both approaches have made some contribution, Thomas and Ely (1996) suggest a third paradigm, *a learning-and-effectiveness paradigm,* which can have more substantive and long-term effects.

> These organizations recognized that employees frequently make decisions and choices at work that draw upon their cultural background—choices made because of their identity-group affiliations. The companies have also developed an outlook on diversity that enables them to *incorporate* employees perspectives into the main work of the organization and enhance work by rethinking primary tasks and redefining markets, products strategies, missions, business practices, and even cultures. Such companies are using the learning-and-effectiveness paradigm for managing diversity and, by doing so, are tapping diversity's true benefits. (Thomas & Ely, 1996, pp. 85–86)

Based on this learning and effectiveness paradigm, Thomas (1996) proposes a *three-phase model* that is concise, comprehensive, and easily understood. The first step, called *"talking the talk,"* is when top administration and senior managers are introduced to the concept of diversity. This top leadership cohort must acknowledge its willingness to embrace this process of change, which entails committing the necessary resources to this initiative and working to put an organizational structure in place for implementation.

The second step, *"thinking the talk,"* builds on this work of securing conceptual clarity and requires relating the concept of diversity to the organization's mission, vision, and culture. It means exploring current organizational assumptions by conducting an actual assessment of prevailing attitudes and behaviors of the organizational members in relation to diversity as well as the practices of the institution. This "cultural audit" (Thomas, 1991) offers rich information not only about the current situation but, more importantly for the assessment, about the historical practices and policies that serve as the root generators of the current culture. Thus efforts to move an organization from Level 2 to Level 3 requires an understanding of why a Level 2 culture exists.

For example, reported words such as "this company is like a family" may signal an organization in which the top administrators are seen as the parental authorities, in which managerial supervisors are viewed as the responsible older children, and in which all other employees are treated as the younger siblings (Thomas, 1991, p. 52). Inherent in this maxim may be forms of "father knows best," "loyalty above all," and "boys will be boys," values that are then often reflected in the organization's structure, its system of promotion and mentoring, as well as its rewarded behaviors. Thomas asserts that this type of organization probably is supportive of individuals who are most similar to top administration and adverse to heightened diversity with its different cultural norms and mores.

Once the cultural audit is completed, management should be ready to specify the change that is needed and to prioritize actions for these changes. It is at this point that education and training activities may occur to provide all staff in the organization with the opportunity to learn and try out new behaviors and skills.

The final step is *"walking the talk,"* which includes constantly monitoring and measuring progress for feedback about the diversity process. Changes in the organizational culture are made and remade in response to a dialogue among members about the actual progress made and possibilities for continuous improvement as original goals for change are met.

Although these three steps in this action model of organizational diversity progression are not necessarily sequential, there is an understandable logic to their flow. "Good preparation makes for easier doing; where ample attention has been given to talking and thinking, walking is relatively straightforward" (Thomas, 1996, p. 233). Thomas cites an example from the for-profit sector in which the senior executives of General Motors have made an expressed commitment to the active management of diversity (Thomas, 1996, p. 127). They view this as a broad commitment that "extends beyond the door of our company. It includes our leaderships, our suppliers, and the many communities where we operate" (p. 237). Their next step was to conduct a cultural audit. This example resonates with experiences within nonprofit human service organizations whose missions are directly related to, and often inclusive of, diversity concerns (Gant, 1996; Gant & Guitierrez, 1996; Guitierrez, 1992).

In sum, to ensure more progress with diversity in human service agencies in the future requires educating and securing the active engagement of the organizations' leaders. Movement toward Level 4 will occur only if administrators and managerial supervisors believe it will foster the organizational mission. It then requires them to purposefully and thoughtfully work together to create an institutional culture that rewards the differences while honoring the similarities among staff.

A TYPOLOGY OF PERSONAL ORIENTATIONS TO DIVERSITY

Although most of the literature on diversity has focused on the stages of an organization's development, the development and change within an organization are directly related to the behavior of the individual members involved. A typology of levels of individual orientations that parallels the organizational ones is also useful.

Decker (1988), whose work focuses on the interpersonal art of communication, builds on Maslow's typology of stages of human development. He identifies the following levels of individual orientations that can serve to facilitate the supervision of individual workers and assist supervisors in recognizing the different levels of diversity awareness and, therefore, the competence of their staff.

Level 1, *unconscious incompetence*, is when individuals are completely insensitive to their attitudes and behaviors and have never thought about the area of concern. This level presents the greatest challenge to the managerial supervisor.

Level 2, *conscious incompetence*, is the first step in the assumption of individual responsibility: the individual professional is aware of the problem, but is unable to deal with it. The transition to this level is often a rude awakening, but an important step in growth and change.

Level 3, *conscious competence*, is an important stage in which individuals are working hard to improve their competence. The challenge here is to support the growth and explore options and approaches for more effective performance.

Level 4, *unconscious competence*, the goal of diversity work, is when the professional has built in appropriate awareness and sensitivity, and intuitively is effective with colleagues and clients.

Chatterjee (1998) has a similar typology, but he suggests other levels of involvement that are more complex and that managerial supervisors must be prepared to handle. The level of *active resistance or even opposition* to diversity is one in which staff members are not open to growth. Consequently their professional performance in relation to their clients may be seriously affected and the ensuing performance evaluation could have strong negative consequences. Chatterjee also suggests two other levels wherein individuals *patronize diversity* or *talk diversity*, but their actions are not consistent with their words. His final level, in which people *practice diversity* (i.e., verbally and through their actions, they value and promote diversity) is compatable with Decker's levels of conscious competence or unconscious competence.

Comerford (1998) affirms that adults tend to learn about self and other similarities and differences through a personal investment of emotions that necessitates maintaining an open mind and being present oriented. Her work is important when working at both the individual and organizational levels. Comerford (pp. 119–157) identifies 10 constructs that collectively support learning about diversity: exposure (having contact with and knowing about the "other"), engagement (having interactions and joining with "others" to intentionally learn about one another), emotion (opening one's self up to "feel"), empathy (having the capacity to connect with another through "feeling" the other), story-telling (sharing lived experiences among one another), the holding environment (having active support from one's family and peers), personal disposition (having the capacity to stay open and vulnerable to the process of learning about self and other), and the learning environment (having the actual time, space, and presence of colearners working together to create a culture rich with opportunities for learning about diversity).

Understanding personal views and behaviors toward diversity is critical for managerial supervisors. However, it is necessary for managerial supervisors to identify their own level of competence before they can work with other staff to recognize theirs.

CHALLENGES IN IMPLEMENTING DIVERSITY PROGRAMS

As we explore the challenges we should make explicit the costs and benefits of fully promoting diversity in the workplace. There is an extensive literature in this area (Adelman, 1997; Champagne 1997; Griessman, 1993; Myers, 1997; Zuniga, 1997).

As a start it is useful to explore the benefits of diversity programs. Although many are obvious, it is useful to make them explicit:

- Supporting diversity helps the human service organization achieve its mission.

- Supporting diversity by enhancing self-awareness and providing education helps eliminate stereotypes and prejudices toward staff and clients. This work must begin with a self-assessment since managerial supervisors cannot facilitate the growth of their staff without first working on their own development.

- Supporting diversity facilitates increased cooperation and collaboration, essential in the work of interdisciplinary teams. Positive familiarity breeds a degree of comfort and ease that, in turn, provides fertile ground for shared experiences.

- Supporting diversity provides opportunities for dialogue in which honest exchanges of ideas, fears, and questions promote the creation of new insights.

- Supporting diversity acknowledges multiple voices and viewpoints as people recognize differences. Managerial supervisors must not deny the existence of differences nor attempt to homogenize the workplace. Trust is developed through the affirmation of the diverse experiences and perceptions of staff.

- Supporting diversity uncovers various and often unrecognized talents and resources. This allows supervisory managers to more creatively construct work teams that can use the multiple talents for addressing organizational issues.

- Supporting diversity promotes increased flexibility of thought and broader perspectives about the world while reducing judgmental thoughts and actions.

- Supporting diversity may prompt changes in policies and practices that ensure equity through shared participatory managerial arrangements, critical in helping human service organizations approach Level 4 of organizational development.

However, it must be clearly acknowleged that programs that support diversity involve a series of costs, both on an individual and an organizational level.

- Supporting diversity involves a complex learning process that requires the organization to invest in the process through the commitment of time, energy, and money.

- Supporting diversity threatens comfort levels for many people who are initially uncomfortable in dealing with difference. The fear of being prejudged, criticized, ostracized, and devalued are powerful forces that managerial supervisors must recognize.

- Supporting diversity promotes the potential for confrontation, conflict, and even violence as human service organizations begin to dismantle their socially stratified arrangements. This situation may be unavoidable, and managerial supervisors must help their staff use and work through these painful emotions and actions.

- Supporting diversity can accentuate differences, enhance an "us versus them" attitude, and promote feelings of separateness.

Since diversity issues focus on both differences and commonalities, effective managers must recognize and use the existence of both patterns to create an organizational culture in search of wholeness. Recognizing this wholeness facilitates getting beyond the dichotomy of difference and similarity, but it takes time.

Yes, supporting diversity in human service organizations is resource dependent, difficult, and never ending. Managerial supervisors should help staff to realize that this work is always incomplete and unfinished. It is the commitment to the process that reaps the rewards of enhanced growth and productivity. Supervisory managers must know and help their staff realize that when they choose this work as part of the professional journey toward an organizational goal, the journey itself is the work (Gallos, Ramsey, & Associates, 1997).

IMPLEMENTATION: TWO CASE EXAMPLES

In the opening of this chapter we described The Neighborhood Health Center and Visiting Nurse Service whose Executive Director recognized the need to help staff be more effective in the area of diversity.

The approach used was multipronged. First, there was a needs assessment conducted with the staff in which all staff levels were included in focus groups. Second, there was a concentrated training program offered over a 6-month period that began at the executive level and was followed by all staff in mixed groups. There were two or three training sessions a week until all the staff had particpated in at least a 1-day session. This was followed by a staff evaluation of the process with recommendations for the next steps. The outcome was the creation of a Diversity Council for the agency; the consultant led a 1-day retreat with the new Council to help it get organized, to formulate its mission and goals, and to develop a work plan. It was understood that the consultant would be used as the Council developed its work, and a long-term organizational commitment was thus institutionalized.

This illustrates the *learning-and-effectiveness paradigm* proposed by Thomas and Ely (1996), and confirmed by Amey-Taylor (1998) as an optimal model for diversity training. The further work that can be done, once a long-term organizational commitment is made, can include training, counseling with individual managers, working with affinity groups, examining recruitment and retention policies and procedures, developing a newsletter that serves both an educational and cohesiveness function, celebratory events, and a mentoring system. Amey-Taylor (1998) views evaluation as critical, and notes that although much is qualitative information, it is possible to obtain quantifiable, measureable information as well (e.g., recruitment and retention figures, promotional activities, exit interview information). This links directly to our discussion of program evaluation.

A second approach to diversity implementation is the use of Intergroup Dialogue, Education, and Action (IDEA) (Nagda et al., 1997). Within the professional setting, intergroup dialogue offers an approach to engage professionals from different backgrounds in substantive, sustained, and conceptually integrated learning experiences, thus illustrating the applications of the concepts of similarities and difference discussed earlier. The goals of the intergroup dialogue are to encourage the creation of an empathetic self, to heighten one's self-awareness as well as one's awareness of others vis-à-vis social group identities and status, to facilitate critical thinking and knowledge of social inequalities, to develop constructive communication and conflict competencies, to produce a commitment to challenge barriers to positive intergroup relations, and to increase participation in multicultural coalitions. Vehicles to accomplish these goals would include having consistent and ongoing meetings of staff guided by operating principles of candor, confidentiality, and mutual respect, and group activities consisting of role plays and experiential exchanges.

This approach coincides with core social work values of empowerment, found in many human service organizations: building connections with others, increasing critical consciousness about social inequalities, engendering commitments to social justice, and developing competencies to engage in social change. This approach is useful as it generates the creation of common understandings among the participants of the dialogue.

Organizations are beginning to understand that there is a yearning for support and connectedness in arenas in which much of the working day is spent (Shaffer & Anundsen, 1993). IDEA presents a unique opportunity to build a community of caring and understanding within an organizational structure in which there is all too often little or no awareness of the strength of diversity within the workforce.

Human service organizations increasingly have to respond to a changing and diverse clientele and workforce, thus requiring a rethinking and restructuring of approaches to both direct services and management within the organization. In this regard, the Level 3 and Level 4 culturally competent organizations are instructive as they value diversity, have the capacity for self-assessment, are conscious of the dynamics inherent when cultures interact, have institutional cultural knowledge, and have developed processes of working effectively in diverse settings (Cross, 1988).

Intergroup dialogues provide a mechanism for proactive and preventive work in creating responsive, healthy, and culturally sensitive work cultures, as well as providing a problem-solving vehicle for conflict resolution. In the beginning stages of the development of a culturally competent organization, intergroup dialogues can help engender a climate of safety, trust, and respect that allows participants to engage in what otherwise could be difficult and uncomfortable interactions. The process affords opportunities for individual members to uncover and articulate who they are as individuals and begin to discover subtle yet important values that lie below the surface and influence their work lives.

Embedded in this journey of common understanding is uncovering unique histories and current political relationships that inform and influence members' ways of being and working within the organization. Through this process culturally prescribed patterns of communication, etiquette, and problem solving become evident and can provide invaluable tools for future work.

Within an organization in which careful attention has been paid to building a culturally competent system, processes of problem solving and conflict resolution are more naturally facilitated by intergroup dialogue. In essence, once the foundation of trust, safety, and respect has been developed, the stage is set to allow intergroup dialogues to process difficult situations and arrive at mutually acceptable resolutions based on consensus. This process is directly related to the managerial tensions that are discussed in relation to whistleblowers, unions, and downsizing in Chapter 9.

A natural auxiliary benefit is the role modeling this provides for workers within the organization to utilize this approach in working with their clients and their communities. Managerial supervisors must recognize that intergroup dialogues require a consistent and on-going commitment to provide the support, time, and resources to ensure that individuals feel valued and affirmed in this process.

Preliminary evaluation results of IDEA show that participants increased their commitment to cultural diversity and became more critically aware of their own experiences and the experiences of others. Discussing controversial issues in a constructive manner empowered IDEA participants to take actions against injustices.

CONCLUSION

It is our hope that managerial supervisors will find these examples of implementation useful as they seek approaches for moving their departments forward on the continuum of diversity awareness and promotion. However, as noted throughout this chapter, managerial supervisors and their human service organizations will be well served by first assessing their organization's level of support for diversity and then acknowledging the costs and benefits of this work. Managers can then begin to learn how to teach their staff to deal with the paradoxical tensions of uniqueness and similarity. Giving staff the time, space, and opportunity to develop themselves and their structures is a must for effective managerial supervision in doing diversity work.

Fnally it must be noted that there are no simple answers, no clear-cut processes in embarking on this journey. It is an ongoing challenge that requires continuous adjustment and readjustment within the organizational context.

7

Creating and Sustaining Interdisciplinary Teams

The presence of informal work groups in human service organizations is probably as old as the first organization. Certainly human service professionals have long valued teamwork in health care, education, mental health, and other settings. Managerial supervisors play unique and important roles in the development and sustenance of teams. The push for *interdisciplinary* teaming can be linked to the professionals' desire to view clients holistically, to the organization's need to clarify lines of communication and authority, and even to external policies in which third party payers encourage team approaches to the provision of care (Vinokur-Kaplan, 1994).

A long-term care rehabilitation team that was formed in a local health care system to work with disabled patients illustrates an appropriate organizational response to the needs of patients. The team was seen as a way to promote quality care and to ensure that all the appropriate disciplines were involved in the planning and delivery of appropriate care. Members of the team came from the following disciplines: medicine, nursing, occupational therapy, physical therapy, and social work. The team leader was the director of the social work unit and had extensive experience in working with teams in other settings.

In this chapter we take a close look at interdisciplinary teams, with the managerial supervisor as team leader and highlight some of the critical intrateam issues. Our discussion will be related to the team described above in order to elucidate the theoretical content. An interesting paradox exists in this situation that must be dealt with in managerial supervision: *just as persons need to be competent autonomous individual professionals trained in their respective disciplines, they must simultaneously function well in interdisciplinary groups that are interdependent, mutual, and reciprocal.*

WHAT IS A TEAM?

In the 1940s a shift in orientation in management studies and practice occurred from the scientific management approach to the human relations school of thought. Not only did managers now recognize that satisfying workers' needs for socialization could be a source of reward, they also realized that formal work groups could also be powerful tools in expediting organizational change (The Slade Company Case, 1960). In the 1950s one of the first books on interdisciplinary teams was written that highlighted factors, still relevant today, to be considered by managerial supervisors as they work with teams (Luszki, 1958).

Teams are not new. There is a general interest in project teams, task teams, multidisciplinary teams, and interdisciplinary teams, which assumes that teams contribute to quality performance. Popular management concepts such as Total Quality Management and restructuring strategies such as Reengineering are grounded in teaming. Hammer (1996) asserts that

One does not make a group of individuals a team simply by declaring them to be one. It takes training and learning, and even then the path is not an easy one. There will inevitably be friction and conflicts. . . . Despite the current popularity of the team concept, most people in contemporary organizations have virtually no experience working in teams. (p. 84)

Definitions of teams abound in the literature, all distinctly complementing the other. Whereas Shipka (1997) focuses on the simple definition of teams as a web of relationships, Bulin (1995) expands this concept as she describes teams "as a group of people who are interdependent and who recognize that the success of each one of them hinges on the success of the group. It is more than just a number of people acting together; as a group, it has evolved to its highest level of development" (p. 125), performing its tasks most effectively. Katzenbach and Smith (1993) further expand the definition: "A team is a small number of people with complementary skills who are committed to a common purpose, performance goals, and an approach for which they hold themselves mutually accountable" (p. 45). Thus we can define teams as groups of people who work together toward common goals and objectives in almost every health and human service organization in this country.

But what makes a team interdisciplinary? Certainly multiple disciplines are involved in teaming, but each discipline can actually be somewhat removed and remote, present but not integrated. And this distinguishes multidisciplinary groups from interdisciplinary ones. Interdisciplinary teaming requires that these multiple disciplines actually work together on a common problem, that they engage in some cross-training, and that they come to a common solution or strategy as an integrated group. This is not easy. "In contrast to multidisciplinary teamwork, interdisciplinary teamwork is characterized by shared purpose, creative problem solving, and synergy in which combined activities result in a product greater than the individual components" (Fatout & Rose, 1995, p. 51). It takes work and talent on the part of managerial supervisors to support and nurture effective interdisciplinary teaming.

In the case discussed above, the team leader had to make clear that members of all of the disciplines were valued participants in the group process, and that the effective outcome of every case plan depended on the expertise of all involved. Given the traditional dominance of the medical profession, particularly in a hospital setting, this required sensitive leadership on the part of the managerial supervisor who had to simultaneously support all the participants while attending to the needs of physicians in relation to what was for them a new role.

It should be noted that whether we are studying time-limited project teams designed to perform a specific task or ongoing work teams designed to share multiple tasks with responsibility for entire products, as in our case, "a team approach is required where simultaneity of observation is necessary" (Luszki, 1958, p. 11). This means that more than one discipline must actually experience and assist in interpreting what is happening because it takes more than one perspective to solve some of the complex problems that occur in the human services.

USE OF THE TEAM

Knowing when, how, and why to use a team is fundamental to the effectiveness of the team and the organization, and central to the role of the managerial supervisor. Since teams are often viewed as a panacea in today's human service environment, it is too easy to view everything from a team perspective. It is important to point out that it is never an either/or situation: there will be times when an individual can more appropriately perform certain functions that do not require a full team effort.

For example, the physical therapist previously described in our long-term care rehabilitation team has a clear individual role to play in working with the patient who is close to discharge, and must constantly determine the goals and approaches to be used in the physical therapy situation. The physical therapist's contribution to the team discussion provides the information that is needed by all of the members in order to formulate an appropriate plan that takes into account Medicare coverage and next steps once Medicare terminates its coverage.

The team leader must come to a decision regarding when, how, and why to use an interdisciplinary team. In considering the formation of a team, the leader must take into account several elements. First is the appropriateness of the team "when there is need for the integration of different perceptual fields, or for the interrelation of a series of different sorts of observations made by different persons on the same object" (Luszki, 1958, p. 11). However, of equal importance is the selection of individuals who potentially will be effective team members. These are people who are secure in their professional identities and yet dissatisfied with the limits of their own profession; these individuals are described as "discovery minded" and not status or reward seeking. They enjoy the prospect of being challenged by the other professions' perspectives, seeing teaming as an opportunity for their own "real growth and development" (Luszki, 1958, pp. 199–205).

Given this profile of an effective interdisciplinary team member, managerial supervisors work to build a community of interests in which members more strongly identify with the team's goals than with the goals of any of the individual disciplines. This requires an atmosphere that encourages open, free discussion while at the same time supporting loyalty to both the team member's own profession and the work of the team. Managerial supervisors can be helped to work with their teams if they recognize that teams are specialized project groups and that the literature on working with groups can be most helpful (Schopler & Galinsky, 1995; Wheelan, 1994).

TEAM LEADERSHIP

Team leadership is the keystone for all team activities. It necessitates "the articulation of a vision, the creation of a clear mission, and the development of goals, objectives, and action plans" for the team (Parker, 1990, p. 99). In this discussion we will focus on the team leader's role in managing the relationship between the team and the larger institution, in facilitating the stages in the development of the team, and in serving as coach and team advocate.

MANAGING THE TEAM/ORGANIZATION INTERFACE

An exploration of some of the major organizational challenges facing teams is necessary to understand the leadership role performed by the managerial supervisor. The team leader is the boundary spanning gatekeeper, the bridge between the team and the larger organization. Managerial supervisors must therefore ensure that their role has legitimacy in the organization and that the administration openly acknowledges the importance of both the leader and the team. This is a reciprocal process in that the administration's support provides the important base for the team's success in achieving its goals. This, in turn, increases the power of the leader in the team and the position of influence of the leader in the larger organization.

In the case of the long-term care rehabilitation team, its effectiveness is largely dependent on the sanction of the health care system's administration. This is related not only to the working relationships that must be developed among the various departments, but also to billing and insurance as well as discharge planning.

However, it is not an automatic process: the orientation needed by the central administration about interdisciplinary teams requires ongoing attention for the lifetime of the team. Information to be given includes identifying when teams are appropriate, what they can accomplish, which disciplines need to be involved at which times, and what the teams will require from the organization. It is important to also continuously emphasize that creating and sustaining effective teams require a commitment of organizational resources, but when the goal is attained it is more robust and comprehensive in scope and depth than if it were obtained by an individual effort. It must be emphasized that the management of time is a critical function of team leadership and sufficient time must be allotted for all the various aspects of teamwork. Inadequate or interrupted time leads only to frustration, which may become fertile ground for unnecessary and unproductive intrateam conflict and inefficiency and ineffectiveness in the organization.

Serving as a bridge is not a one-way process. Just as the organization's administration requires ongoing orientation about the team, the team also requires ongoing orientation about the organization. Thus the manager must help the team understand the organization's needs and limitations in meeting all of the team's requirements. Team members' lenses should not be myopic.

Managerial supervisors must ensure that the appropriate flow of tangible and intangible resources goes into the team and that the necessary amount of new information flows between the team and the organization. Too few resources can starve a team's effort whereas too much information can overwhelm the team. Both realities can render the team ineffective.

Managing the interface between the team and the organization requires managerial supervisors to understand the cultures of both in order to translate and relay information and work toward the best interests of both. The most effective managers use this form of bicultural competency to strategically advocate for the team while building sociopolitical capital within the organization. The degree of managerial effectiveness here relies not only on an understanding of the knowledge, skills, and values implicit in the process but also on the ability of managerial supervisors to use their political skills and position within the larger organization. Managerial supervisors should recognize that it is natural that persons who are external to the team may see it as diminishing the identity and expertise of a particular profession, particularly since the leader's discipline will always differ from many of the team members. Consequently, the supervisor must be respected not only within the team but also within the larger organization, and must be viewed as a professional who explicitly values and supports the contributions of the different professions within the context of the larger organization.

The best public relations and morale-boosting statement for interdisciplinary teams is the achievement of the attained goal. The organization's administration will need the managerial supervisor to assist in incorporating the team's outcomes into the core operations of the organization. All this hard work will be worth the effort if the team's attained goal becomes part of what is recognized as contributing to making the organization successful.

FACILITATING TEAM DEVELOPMENT

Teams undergo stages of development like other groups (Bion, 1959; Bennis & Shepard, 1961; Schutz, 1966; Wheelan, 1994). Effective managerial supervisors must monitor and guide the team's development process. Following earlier models, Wheelan and Hochberger (1996) propose a stage model of team development that can inform the team leader's strategy to intervene and facilitate appropriately. The model features five stages: dependency and inclusion, counterdependency and fight, trust and structure, work and productivity, and termination. Awareness of common group dynamics in any of these stages can be essential to successful leadership and group development overall.

The first stage—dependency and inclusion—is "characterized by members' significant dependency on the designated leader, by concerns about safety, and by inclusion issues" (p. 76). The leader's role at this point is to facilitate members' actual, versus "pseudo," engagement in the work at hand, and the group process as a whole. Particular attention needs to be paid to ensuring group members' experience of safety while still inviting them to actively participate, as they negotiate issues of authority and membership.

Stage two—counterdependency and fight—is a natural point at which "the group seeks to liberate itself from its dependence on the leader" (p. 76). Some struggle is likely to ensue among group members about goals and how the group is going to be run. Contrary to any impulse to diffuse conflict, it is important to accept it at this stage as part of the process. "The group's task at this stage is to develop a unified set of goals, values, and operational procedures . . . [which] inevitably generates conflict, which is also necessary for the establishment of trust and a climate in which members feel free to disagree with each other" (p. 76).

The third stage—trust and structure—signifies the group's ability to resolve conflict and become more focused on the tasks for which the team is meant to convene. Cooperation, negotiation, and more open communication about tasks, roles, and procedures are the hallmarks of this stage. "It is also a time during which members work to solidify positive relationships with one another" (p. 77).

Work and productivity—the fourth stage—is the period when the resolutions of the earlier stages allow the team to focus on the work at hand. The energy available to the team is used more productively and effectively for achievement of its intended goals.

The final stage—termination—is an essential aspect of team

process. When groups have a designated ending point, this stage becomes more obvious, but less definitive transition points may also evoke similar patterns (e.g., the end of a particular project, or the departure of members of the team). The patterns likely to emerge at this stage include the reenactment of earlier conflicts, as well as a more reflective assessment of the work accomplished by the team. The role of the leader at this point is to anticipate and facilitate the termination process, rather than let it go unaddressed.

It is important to note that, as with any stage theory, human process is not always as linear as the model may infer. Therefore, the team leader in particular must recognize that group process (including movement through the five stages) varies, may be non-linear, and may also be confounded by either internal or external factors. As Hochberger and Wheelan (1996) point out, "depending on the circumstances and forces affecting the group at any given moment, group dynamics may fluctuate widely. . . . In the rapidly changing, volatile healthcare environment, many of these conditions that negatively influence team effectiveness are prevalent and place even more obstacles in the path of the . . . team struggling to work together" (p. 77). Since teamwork in today's social services environment usually relies on on-the-job training in group dynamics, it becomes the responsibility of the team leader to facilitate the group development process.

Institutionalizing the goal and celebrating the team's accomplishments are critical steps in the team's work as it moves from one problem to the next. Managerial supervisors must work with the administration to publicly recognize the importance of the goal that was achieved, to praise the team, and to show the connection between the achieved goal and the broader organization's improved performance.

If the team is a short-term, problem-oriented one, the task of adjourning the team and managing the final aspect of the team/organization interface is the remaining important role of the managerial supervisor (Bailey, 1991). This helps the members of the team as they move back into their traditional roles and working relationships, and ensures a continuing positive relationship between them and the traditional organizational units.

DESIGNING, COACHING, AND ADVOCATING

In addition to managing the team/organization interface and facilitating team development, team leadership takes a number of forms: designing, coaching, and advocating. *Designing* means that the manager is ultimately responsible for how effective the team's work processes are. If the design does not work, it is the responsibility of the manager to work with team members to change the process, to redesign the program, to make it work.

The *coaching* role is one in which the managerial supervisor is available to the team to provide support in all the processes performed. This does not mean being dictatorial, but it means being available as needed for expertise or outside resources and always being fully cognizant about the team's process. The coaching of teams takes skills in diplomacy, knowing when to intervene and when to observe.

As an *advocate* for the team, the managerial supervisor interfaces with others in the organization, not only serving as a supportive buffer with the organization but also advocating for the implementation and institutionalization of the team's work. Thus the managerial supervisor has a great responsibility in representing the interests of the team.

WORKING WITH TEAM MEMBERS

The managerial supervisor has an active role in organizing the team. It consists of determining the composition of the team, selecting and orienting the members, ensuring open communication, helping to build trust, providing support, and managing differences among the team. Determining the appropriate composition of the team is a critical management activity, since teams vary depending on the problems they are addressing. Usually the first task of management is integrating a complement of members' skills and members' potential to best meet the challenges of the team's work. In addition, a key task is to identify potential new team leaders among this new cohort and to help them to develop their capacities with appropriate training and leadership opportunities.

Luszki (1958) identifies four individual characteristics that must be considered when building a team. The most successful team members are individuals who are interested in the team's purpose, who have the ability to recognize the interrelatedness of many different factors, who have had at least one prior positive team experience, and who demonstrate the appropriate "temperament" and motivation for teaming (pp. 197–205). Bennis and Shepard (1961) note that these characteristics can be divided into two categories: task functions (i.e., the knowledge needed to complete the tasks) and maintenance functions (i.e., the interpersonal abilities needed to help the team elicit and use the knowledge to keep the team working). The first two characteristics on Luszki's list are more task-oriented functions whereas the last two are more maintenance-oriented functions. Ideally, all members can contribute skills to both of these areas.

SELECTING AND ORIENTING TEAM MEMBERS

The most obvious, yet the most critical, element of any team is the member's degree of clarity about and commitment to the team's purpose. Luzski (1958, p. 272) emphasized that a strong identification with the team's purpose was the most important factor of effective teamwork, and managerial supervisors must continuously remind the team of its reason for existence. Keeping the team's purpose in front of the group serves as a motivator and a reminder of at least one shared value within the team. Supervisors must also ensure that team members know exactly why they are a part of the team and understand their individual contribution. These actions are necessary not only in the start-up or "forming" days of the team but also in the development of its internal ordering, referred to as the "norming" phase (Bailey, 1991).

ENSURING OPEN COMMUNICATION

Open communication is a necessity, and relates directly to Chapter 5, "Facilitating Communication." Team members must know that their ideas, questions, and even confusions are valued within the team. This means honest, but focused, communication between team members and supervisors. Supervisors can best model this component by bringing their suggestions to the team and, equally importantly, by explaining their new or recurring frustrations and misunderstandings. This requires managerial supervisors to be skillful in giving and receiving feedback. Feeling encouraged to express themselves, members can develop an understanding of how their team provides for this exchange of authenticity and appropriate openness. Creating a culture in which teams can ask for clarification and feel comfortable with confrontation is the managerial supervisor's responsibility.

Managerial supervisors have a critical role to play in helping persons from diverse disciplines to understand each other and also to find the benefits of working together to meet client needs.

BUILDING MUTUAL TRUST AND SUPPORT

It is easy to see how trust and openness are interdependent; the existence of one facilitates the existence of the other. Moreover, when the presence of trust and openness is acknowledged and valued, even greater degrees of trust and openness are generated. Managerial supervisors must remember that trust that is highly dependent on behaviors, and not just words, can be easily destroyed. The ability to acknowledge mistakes and even to apologize for inadvertently offending team members is important for all members of an effective team and is critical for managerial supervisors. This requires that managerial supervisors have an appreciation of their own self-worth especially in the context of the team: supervisors who are insecure in their role are limited in their ability to develop a climate of trust and openness.

As with trust and openness, the existence of supportive interactions among team members is part of the norm of effective teaming. Managerial supervisors who are supportive provide an important model for team members, enhancing their ability to be supportive to one another. Acts of overt compassion, care, and assistance are necessary elements for mutual support to occur. The managerial supervisor must ensure that the team has the necessary resources of time and space to devote to these types of interactions, which take time to be developed. Ideally, mutual support should not be just an expectation for the team, but should be mirrored in the entire organizational culture.

Managing Differences

If all the above elements are evident within a team, members will feel safe enough to allow controversial opinions, challenging questions, and individually held values to surface. However, it is essential that adequate time be allocated from the very begining to allow this to take place. In the preceding chapter we dealt with the role of the managerial supervisor in valuing diversity; that content is equally important to team development and growth. Furthermore, we know that it is essential that the team work through what has been called the *storming* phase of its development, often related to the management of differences. Only if these differences are openly acknowledged and dealt with, will the team be able to be effective in achieving its goal (Tuchman & Jensen, 1977). This is also related to the challenges of dealing with and confronting conflict, discussed in Chapter 5, "Facilitating Communication."

Managerial supervisors must have a high degree of self-awareness that allows them to be able to differentiate their own disciplinary assumptions, and even biases, from those other disciplinary viewpoints among team members. The ability to recognize and then work through individual personal and professional "isms" is critical to teaming. However, this does not mean that managerial supervisors suppress expressions of competition due to difference. Rather, they must work with team members to determine the appropriate degrees of competition *and* cooperation necessary to allow the team to tolerate differences and then use the differences to further strengthen the team (Luszki, 1958). Managerial supervisors must allow time for the team to discuss its process for making decisions as well as its procedures for resolving conflict and creating consensus. They must also work to help all of the team members be able to use both process and content in team meetings.

THE PARADOX OF RELATIONSHIP

We believe that much of team interaction is nested within the management of what we call the paradox of relationship. As discussed in the beginning of this chapter, this paradox consists of the need for individual professional growth, development, performance competence, and autonomy in contrast to the team's need for interdependence and mutuality. Technical skills, textbook knowledge, and a pro-team value base aside, truly effective interdisciplinary teams require first an acknowledgment of this paradox and then an understanding of how to manage it. Like all other paradoxes, this one is made up of competing realities and simultaneous opposites. Although paradoxes do not have to be resolved, they must be managed (Handy, 1994).

The seeds for understanding the paradox of relationship are within the relational model of growth and development. This model emphasizes the role of interactions in which adult growth is viewed not merely as outgrowing dependency but rather as a process that develops increasingly complex forms of interdependency (Miller, 1991). An examination of the three central elements of relational interactions, interdependence, mutuality, and reciprocity, provides a deeper understanding of the relationship paradox and suggests possible ways to manage it.

Interdependence, rather than autonomy, is the ideal state of development according to the relational model. Implicit in this statement is the belief that dependence on others for self-identity and self-actualization is half of the growth continuum; the other half is realizing that identity and actualization of the "self" occur when one contributes to the growth of the "other." *Mutuality* is the belief in the two-directional process of development. Achieving mutuality depends on the ability of the "self" *and* the "other" to be both the enabler/mentor *and* the enabled/mentee. *Reciprocity* is the knowledge that both parties have the necessary skills, knowledge, and desire to achieve this bidirectional relationship. Enacting reciprocity requires transcending the boundaries between the state of dependence and the state of independence. This theoretical formulation suggests that both the "self" and "other" continuously move back and forth between these states, thus giving and receiving the benefits of relational interactions.

These elements suggest ways to begin to manage this paradox. First, interdisciplinary teams can foster interdependence *and* autonomy. Effective teams recognize their intraconnections and see their shared values and commitment to the team's purpose as the implicit glue that holds the team together. Members realize that the ability of the team to achieve its goals is dependent on the integration of strength of the individuals. It follows, therefore, that members must retain appreciation for their individual contributions to the team. The degree of self-worth as a team member relies heavily on the appreciation for their individual contributions to the team. To facilitate the balancing of these competing realities, managerial supervisors have to create team cultures that reward risk taking and an openness to change. Addressing the stereotypes that exist within all organizations and among all disciplines will begin to tear down the isolating walls of professionalism.

Second, truly effective interdisciplinary teams focus on their internal operations *and* their external products and/or services. This simultaneous attention to both the "inside" and the "outside" of the team is critical to recognizing changes in needed areas of knowledge and skills among the members. This information enables managerial supervisors to recruit the appropriate new members to enable the team to adequately counter the challenges inherent to achieving the team's goals. These changes in membership, with its concomitant shifts in identifying whose talents are most important to accomplishing the team's tasks at any point in time, require a degree of comfort among members in moving back and forth between teacher and learner roles. Managerial supervisors must help members leave their hierarchical/power differences outside of the team. Additionally, teams often comprise individuals whose reporting hierarchies are often totally unrelated. Managers need to instill a continuous sense of appreciation of meaning and purpose in all members' work regardless of the perceived size or type of their contributions.

Third, interdisciplinary teams require that members learn the language, skills, and the culture of one another's profession while at the same time maintaining their own professional identities. The ability to be both self and other greatly diminishes the gap between disciplines and enables the team to create its own combined language. Supervisors must find ways to recognize and reward the team's work and to acknowledge individuals' contributions. This bilevel system of appraisal embodies the important message of the interplay between the individual professional and the interprofessional team. Managers must also model this relationship of reciprocity by becoming interdisciplinary themselves, not shedding their professional identities, rather interweaving the professions of the many into one's own. Effective managers must be able to risk being both leader–teacher and follower–learner while actively seeking out emerging leaders who know how to be good followers.

DEALING WITH TEAM DYSFUNCTION

So why do some teams not work smoothly or not work at all? Drinka and Streim (1994) offer some insights into why it is so difficult for some teams to function. Beginning with the influence of organizational values, goals, and structure, teams as subunits must fit within the larger host organization. If managers assign people to teams with no provision for giving them much input into their assignments, staff members will feel that they have little or no control over their position within the organization. If the organization provides differential rewards to team members, resentment will fester.

For example, in our case, a member of the rehabilitation team was acting out her own frustrations with the health care system. Other team members were frustrated too, but they were giving every effort to the team, trying to focus on the group goals rather than on their own personal needs. The key offender was the physician on the team who had higher status in the overall medical hierarchy. Finally an explosion occurred in the team meeting; everyone just had too much. Members said things that they regretted later, but one resounding theme emerged. Team members felt that they had no power to dismiss a member of the team, and they felt captive and disempowered. They dreaded team meetings because they knew that their one disgruntled member would dominate and overwhelm them.

Finally, with this honest outburst on the table, the managerial supervisor was able to encourage and support this open expression of conflict and team members began to communicate their views. Until they got to this point, the members felt as if they were living in purgatory (Drinka & Streim, 1994).

Another reason why teams do not always function as planned is directly related to the members' professional training. Certainly professionals are assumed to be competent to perform in their field or discipline, but professionals are not expected to know the roles and skills that other professionals bring to the team. Given the "diverse values, language, methods for problem-solving, and professional behaviors" (Drinka & Streim, 1994, p. 542), it is little wonder that the influence of professional training can actually have a negative impact on teaming. For example, a nurse on a team may interact with other nurses in one way, but discount the social work member of the team. Professional hierarchies and cliques can develop on teams, just as they can in any arena.

The influence of individual background and personal characteristics is interjected into teams as well. As discussed in previous chapters, communication modes and styles can vary greatly. These approaches to the work are learned from childhood and it is likely that repressed emotions will emerge when teams are under stress. Everyone has his or her own way of defending against conflict, and some of these behaviors will be maladaptive. Defensive behavior can interfere with functioning, and dysfunctional dynamics can be highly disruptive. The managerial supervisor must be adept at understanding human behavior and in recognizing when to intervene.

Intervention strategies to ensure effective teamwork are both varied and specific. The managerial supervisor must be clear and consistent in describing the team's orientation, have regularly scheduled meetings that structure interaction, alternate team members as leaders so that ownership is shared, get consultation from the larger system as needed, hold team retreats, foster relationships with other teams by building bridges, use constructive confrontation, and conduct peer reviews in which teams give feedback on their own members (Drinka & Streim, 1994). These various strategies will not only improve the team's functioning but also serve the important function of dealing with, and mitigating, team conflict.

COSTS AND BENEFITS OF TEAMING

The use of interdisciplinary teams in the workplace is a phenomenon that we expect will continue well into the twenty-first century as organizations become better skilled in facilitating and using the synergy of multiple professional ideologies, perspectives, and practices. Much of the literature in the area of organizations and teams (Hackman, 1990; Handy, 1994; Hirschhorn, 1991; Kotter & Heskett, 1992; Shipka, 1997) agrees with the three-part yet very simple analysis offered by Katzenbach and Smith (1993): "First, teams strengthen the performance capability of the individuals, hierarchies, and management processes. . . . Second, teams are practical. And, third, of course teams get results" (pp. 255–256).

A team that is properly created and maintained results in team members who feel accountable not only for themselves but also for each other (McGregor, 1967). Team successes are experienced as individual achievements, which, in turn, serve as a catalyst for increased performance and personal growth. Furthermore, the very existence of teams consisting of individuals from different professional disciplines forces management to reexamine its basic systems (e.g., planning, budgeting, evaluating) to ensure that all organizational members and functions are integral parts of the system.

Working with teams also has its costs. Schindler-Rainman's (1988, pp. 121–122) review of several negative aspects of teams offers a cautionary note to any team manager:

- Team members' commitments may be incompatible.
- Team members may have hidden agendas that interfere with the process.
- Someone may be unable to work as a group member.
- The team may lack clear direction or a sense of purpose.
- The leader may have a laissez-faire attitude.
- Organizational inexperience [with teams] may hinder the process.

- The organization may not support the team as it should.
- Unappreciated and unsupported teams often disintegrate.

An examination of the costs and the benefits of interdisciplinary teams underscores the necessity for skillful managerial supervisors as team leaders, since interdisciplinary teams not only have the potential for greater impact than individuals do but also have greater flexibility than do individual organizational departments. Effective teams thus serve two important purposes: they can provide their individual members with opportunities for recognition, reward, motivation, and personal development and also provide the organization with models for high synergistic performance.

CONCLUSIONS

In summary, interdisciplinary teams have been found to be one of the most effective organizational strategies for responding to and proactively beginning to challenge the rapid, complex changes occurring in both the professions and the environment. Certainly teams have costs and benefits. If correctly created and maintained, with the appropriate leadership and membership, the benefits can far outweigh the costs. Managing teams means dealing with team dysfunction, addressing the paradox of relationship, and providing leadership in the form of designing, coaching, and advocating. Managers and teams alike can work to balance the competing demands placed on their organizational unit and to enhance the potency of the team's work as well.

8

Motivating, Appraising, and Rewarding

In this chapter we look at the interconnection of three primary responsibilities of managerial supervisors in relationship to their staff—motivation, performance appraisal, and reward. We see these activities as essential and interdependent. Therefore, supervisors who want highly effective staff need to understand, and to know how to handle, these processes.

We begin with a brief historical perspective of how people are rewarded in organizations, followed by an overview of understanding motivation. Several different types of performance appraisal systems designed to increase individuals' motivation for effective work become the focus of this chapter since we believe that motivating employees is critical to everything one does in an organization, particularly in the labor-intensive human service context. We then focus on the importance of rewarding positive behavior and of creating a reward-based culture. And finally, we address the paradox inherent in evaluation: *how to balance the need to motivate with the need to evaluate performance.*

HISTORICAL PERSPECTIVES

A quick look back from the turn of the century to the present reveals much about how organizational leadership views and rewards staff. Beginning with scientific management (Taylor, 1911), through the 1920s, people were viewed as rational, nonemotional beings. Only a few were believed to have the capacity to manage. Pay was the most important reward. Without enough pay, people were thought to not work productively. Management's role was to closely plan for, direct, and monitor employees. In the scientific organization the focus was on role relationships instead of personal relations, and on technical efficiency. Rationalization, routinization, and specialization were expected behaviors from workers. Individuals, at this time, were viewed as well-honed instruments and well-trained bodies.

From the 1930s to the mid-1940s, the human relations school of management (Maslow, 1943) was in vogue. Individuals were now recognized as social beings who worked within groups. Relationships were seen as important sources of rewards. It was believed that without caring relationships with management, employees would not work productively. Management's role was to structure work groups, counsel, and understand employees. In the human relations organization, the focus was on the people and their role in the system. It was now thought that the formal organization should offer interventions such as counseling programs, personal attention, and opportunities for group integration.

Theory "Y" management (McGregor, 1960) was popular from the mid-1940s through the 1960s. This approach recognized that individuals seek self-fulfillment; therefore, intrinsic rewards were seen as most important to employees. Organizational leaders believed that the absence of autonomy would dampen interest and that people welcomed challenges and increased responsibility. The leader's role was to organize tasks to promote interest and to manage the mutual setting of work objectives. Planning was viewed as a tool for coordination, not just control. Therefore, deviation from the formal plan was assumed to be either a misunderstanding or a new act on behalf of the organization. Career development was now recognized as an important managerial function and a reward for successful employees.

The contingency approach to management (Fiedler, 1967) was popular from the mid-1960s through the mid-1980s. Individuals were seen as complex beings, with needs that varied, developed, and changed. Appropriate rewards were now viewed as a function of a person's culture, personality, task assignment, and social relationships. Motivation depended on fitting the organizational culture with the tasks to be done and with the people who were involved. The leader's role was to assess situations and provide pragmatic fit among organizational components. In the contingency organization departments were organized differently to respond to varying internal and external environmental demands. Staffing goals were to link people with work specific tasks that fit personalities and work styles. Department differentiation was recognized as creating productive conflict that required complex forms of integration.

In today's multicultural approach, begun in the mid-1980s, individuals are recognized as fluid, capable of change, and arbiters of multiple cultures (Handy, 1994; Sashkin, 1995; Thomas, 1996). Life is seen as a "social construction" of reality (Berger & Luckman, 1967). Dilemma management, the recognition of competing truths rather than right or wrong problems, is the primary focus of the organization. Rewards depend on how workers define the situation. The leader's role is to create and sustain a shared culture that focuses on attention and commitment to organizational goals. In the multicultural organization all are encouraged to be vision oriented. There is a high degree of information sharing and participation in "meaning-making" activities. The organization requires fluid structures and flexible policies to allow for different types of memberships. The human service organization is, therefore, a constantly evolving construction with a broad and changing array of human dialogues.

THE PARADOX OF EVALUATION

The historical perspective just presented provides background for defining a central issue confronting contemporary managerial supervisors who want to motivate and reward and must also appraise their staff. Assumptions in today's human service organizations are that supervisees are both able to be trusted and trust that their supervisors are able to judge their productivity in a fair way. The paradox, of course, is that it would be naive to assume that all supervisory relationships work in such a fair, even-handed, and assertive manner. Accordingly, if a particular individual is unable to fulfill her or his responsibilities—to no longer be effective in the job—then that individual would no longer be entrusted to fulfill that role.

The paradox surrounding evaluation works at every level within the organization. To begin to reconcile this paradox, managerial supervisors must work with agency administrators to create the hiring, motivating, appraising, rewarding, and firing policies and practices that embrace the ideology of the effective organization. It is necessary to inspire confidence and motivation; but that motivation must fit with what is needed to get the work of the organization done. Paradoxically, some employees may be highly motivated, but their energies may be directed toward tasks that do not help the agency get the work done. Managerial supervisors must be skilled at redirecting those energies without reducing employee motivation. This is a great challenge, but evaluation of performance is a reality of organizational life.

MAJOR THEORIES OF MOTIVATION

The literature is replete with theories that offer different insights into what encourages people to be productive, creative, and achieving—to be and do their best on the job. In human service organizations, managerial supervisors must find ways to integrate approaches that they understand and feel comfortable using as they supervise individual staff members within the needs and resources of their unit in the organization. This integration begins with an awareness that there are different theories about motivation. The discussion that follows is designed to illustrate how important it is to recognize the diverse motivations in the workforce.

RECOGNIZING DIVERSE EMPLOYEE NEEDS

Needs theories are based on the premise that identifying individual needs and satisfying individual needs are the most powerful motivators that exist (Alderfer, 1972; Herzberg, Mausner, & Snyderman, 1959; Maslow, 1954; McClelland, 1961). We will describe a few theories focusing on needs that can be useful in managerial supervision.

Maslow's (1954) hierarchy of needs is most frequently cited: the idea that people cannot focus on self-actualization if they do not first have lower order needs met is familar to service professionals and lay persons alike. What this means for managerial supervisors is that they must find ways to create work settings that allow for creativity, self-assessment, and personal and professional growth if they want their employees to be fully motivated (Bryant, 1998).

Two-Factor or Motivator-Hygiene theory divides motivation into two categories (Herzberg et al., 1959). *Motivating factors* include areas of increased responsibility, autonomy, opportunities for advancement, and feelings of achievement. These factors are related to a person's job, and are seen as driving forces behind one's sense of growth and job satisfaction. *Hygiene factors* focus on the work environment and include the level of pay, working conditions, relationships with colleagues, and organizational policies and practices. Hygiene factors are not seen as actually motivating staff; but they are deemed necessary at a level acceptable to staff in order to allow the motivating factors to work. According to this theory, managerial supervisors need to recognize that motivators such as freedom to perform one's job or lots of praise might not be entirely enough if basic factors contributing to economic well-being are not being adequately addressed.

As an example, a small nonprofit agency serving older persons was located in a large southwestern city. This agency was recognized nationally, as it was a leader in providing caregiver training and support for multitudes of people who performed the invisible role of caregiving for elder relatives. Staff, all female, were dedicated persons, many of whom had themselves been caregivers and who understood the potential isolation of performing this role. The agency was composed primarily of paraprofessional staff, with several professional leaders hired to direct specific programs. The energy and excitement among staff at this grassroots agency were almost infectious, but there was an underlying current of tension that grew over the years.

The assumption in this agency's culture was that people would want to be a part of this organization as long as its mission was important to staff. This was true, but some of the staff were single women who could not afford to work for an agency that provided minimal benefits and low pay. This grassroots agency, as it expanded, did not grow in terms of its hygiene factors, even though the motivating factors remained. Staff members began to leave the agency when they could not afford to continue their work there and had to seek employment that adequately addressed their survival needs. The managerial supervisors reported to the board of directors that the agency would suffer as long as the salaries were inadequate, even though the employees were deeply committed to the mission of the agency. Balancing the motivating and the hygiene factors became important in the equation to fully motivate employees to stay. In fact, one supervisor was heard saying, "I think we have finally come of age and we can't act as if everyone should feel priviledged to work here. People feel guilty expressing their needs for reasonable pay and benefits. What's wrong with this culture?"

Another approach to understanding needs is McClelland's (1961) Trichotomy of Needs, which focuses on higher order needs for achievement, affiliation, and power. The now well-known Thematic Apperception Test (TAT) measures these needs. Looking at a series of pictures, individuals describe what they see happening in each picture. This description is therefore viewed as a projection of their needs. For example, viewing a picture of a group of people sitting in a circle as a problem-focused project team would result in receiving a positive score for achievement, reflecting a need to demonstrate competency. Describing the picture as a retirement party would result in receiving a positive score for affiliation, reflecting a need for belonging and relationship. And viewing the same picture as a department meeting that was being run by a department head would result in being scored positively for power, which assumes a need for control of self and others.

This Trichotomy of Needs theory can help managerial supervisors differentiate among possible motivators to identify which incentive is best suited for a particular individual. This requires managerial supervisors to know their supervisees well. For example, many agencies are setting up interdisciplinary teams to deal with highly complex problems. Persons with high power needs are most likely to exert greater influence when they are in charge of a project team rather than simply being a member of the team. This may be a problem if teams are seen as having shared leadership; a person who is motivated by power may actually attempt to dominate the team to the point that others get angry. Contrast this with persons who have high affiliation needs and who may be so concerned with seeking consensus that nothing ever gets done. Affiliation-motivated members might be most satisfied with being an equal member of a team and with enjoying the process of interaction among team members. The managerial supervisor must be sensitive to these two sharply different work styles. For example, overinvolvement with process could totally alienate team members who are achievement oriented and who might feel that nothing ever gets accomplished. A high level of frustration would certainly impede effective performance.

Managers must remember that just as no one theory represents all people, no supervisee's needs can be satisfied by invoking a single theory, since theories usually deal with ideal types. Real people with real jobs are complex, requiring managerial supervisors to motivate their staff through a combination of approaches that best reflects three components: their own styles, the needs of their staff, and the resources of their departments and organizations. Since there is often a turnover among the employees, continuous sensitivity to the needs of the individual supervisee is an ongoing necessity.

Before discussing other motivational areas, we want to emphasize how important it is for managerial supervisors to recognize their own needs. Whereas this discussion has focused on supervisee's needs, managerial supervisors must also have insight into their own motivation. It is important to recognize that one's own needs may be very different from those of others, and that treating employees as one would like to be treated oneself may not always work well. Given the potential for different needs that motivate different persons, the supervisor may find that intervening with a particular employee requires skillful assessment of the needs each of them brings to the job since an interaction between the two is involved.

EQUITY OR SOCIAL COMPARISON

Most people in organizations have heard employees talk about persons who don't "pull their weight." Although it could be argued that all theories of motivation contain an element of this "self-in-relation-to-others" perspective, equity theory is primarily based on individuals' assessments of their own performance and subsequent rewards in comparison to those of others. Equity theory suggests that an individual is motivated by the perceived fairness of the rewards received in relation to the effort exerted (Adams, 1965; Walster, Walster, & Berscheid, 1978). Equity theory asserts that individuals are motivated to reduce any perceived inequities by reducing their own efforts or by reevaluating the efforts of others. Thus employee motivation is based on the employees' perceptions of their own performance, the degree to which they are satisfied with the resulting outcomes, and their satisfaction with the rewards received for those efforts (Nadler & Lawler, 1997; Scott, Farh, & Podsakoff, 1988).

An example from the field illustrates this point.

A nonprofit mental health agency, which was being managed by a for-profit management firm under a 5-year contract, announced a reduction in force. A managerial supervisor, a social worker who worked for the for-profit firm, was responsible for overseeing this unpopular process and received many angry phone calls from the mental health professionals in the agency. This was in response not only to the reduction in force but also to the announcement that the reduction in force would be less if those persons making high salaries would take a small salary cut. Employee expectations, based on past experience, were that their appropriate salaries would increase on a yearly basis. They now felt unappreciated and indignant as a result of the process. The management firm's evaluation of the situation was that if they continued moving in the direction they were going, the agency would be in financial jeopardy.

The MSW supervisor, working from her professional Code of Ethics that emphasized social justice, did not want to begin laying off support persons who were poorly paid; furthermore it would require that many of them would have to be fired in order to make the agency financially viable. By contrast, reducing the salaries of upper level, highly paid mental health personnel by a small amount meant that no one would have to be laid off. Mental health professionals who were normally competent, compassionate people began acting in ways that were highly unprofessional—leaking information to local papers, encouraging clients to complain about the situation, and sending nasty letters to the management firm. Their expectations were that they would continue to be rewarded for their work and the reduction in salary concept was totally foreign to how they had expected to be treated. In the end, five psychiatrists left the agency, angry and unmotivated, to take jobs that actually paid less in other communities. In a way, a reduction in force had been accomplished, but at a tremendous cost to everyone involved.

The managerial supervisor in this situation learned a great deal. She realized that when people are under stress, regardless of how professionally they typically act, they will resort to familiar ways of coping. The psychiatrists saw their livelihoods being threatened and they began to operate in a survival mode. It would have been wise for the supervisor to have invested time in meeting with these professionals in a joint problem-solving process so that communication remained open. Remembering the assumption that communication can be misunderstood might have helped in this situation. This does not mean that the psychiatrists would not have been angry, but they would have at least felt their concerns were being heard. Involving them in the solution does not ensure consensus or harmony, but it does not close the door, inevitably leaving them little alternative but to act out in the larger community—which is exactly what they did.

GOALS AND OBJECTIVES AS MOTIVATORS

The setting of organizational goals and objectives can often serve as a powerful motivator. Goals and objectives define desired end states and staff involvement in the process can lead to higher levels of performance (Eden, 1988; Locke & Latham, 1990).

Goals were emphasized by Drucker (1954) in his Management by Objectives (MBO) approach, in which the process began when leaders established a statement of organizational mission and goals. Department supervisors involved their supervisees in using these goals to set department objectives that collectively worked toward moving the organization forward. McConkey (1975) noted that "managers are more highly committed and motivated when they have definite objectives to work toward, when they know where they're going, when they receive feedback on their performance, when they are judged on results, and when they are rewarded on the basis of results" (p. 95). Not only do these words make intrinsic sense to today's supervisors, but it is readily apparent that these words are also applicable for supervisees. When staff members clearly see how what they do fits with and supports an organization's mission, this awareness alone can serve as a strong motivator for excellent performance. And it can also be noted that this joint effort can be useful in forming the basis on which supervisees' performance is evaluated.

In sum, there are many theories that focus on the what, why, and how of motivation. We have already emphasized the importance of aligning the supervisor's style to the needs and wants of the individual staff and to the needs and resources of the organization while ensuring a cultural norm that provides equity for all. We would be remiss if we did not stress an implicit aspect of motivation. As our workplaces become increasingly more diverse and multicultural, paradoxically so must our motivators become more individualized. What may be perceived as a positive reinforcement to one person or group can be perceived as a punishment to another (e.g., individual praise is not seen as a reward to many of Asian decent or some Native American nations). Similarly, there may be differences in perception of equity (e.g., individuals of Western descent may be more equity sensitive).

Although many variables influence the strength of the goal–performance relationship (e.g., worker's ability, attention to the task, performance feedback from supervisor), good effort leads to good performance and goal setting heightens productivity. Effective supervisors must get to know their staff, both as a collectivity for establishing group-level norms and as individuals with unique needs and expectations.

PERFORMANCE APPRAISAL SYSTEMS

As stated at the outset of this chapter, we believe informing employees about their performance is essential to accomplishing three managerial supervisory responsibilities: maintaining good employer–employee relations, developing and sustaining an effective working organization, and correcting or overcoming employee shortcomings.

Every human service organization evaluates its employees, and in today's world of accountability this is highly necessary. Systems vary tremendously, from informal approaches to very technical, computerized ways of conducting employee performance appraisals. Constructing, maintaining, and updating performance appraisal systems is complicated. Particularly since there is often an absence of clear standards, professional work in the human services is complicated and difficult to evaluate, and, people feel threatened by the process and do not enjoy the prospect of being evaluated.

COMMUNICATING ABOUT PERFORMANCE

One of the primary principles of good supervision is to let each employee know how he or she is getting along. Moreover, employees are usually interested in knowing where they stand with the supervisor. If the employee's work merits a commendation, it should be forthcoming. If the employee's work results are not satisfactory, she or he should know that before receiving disciplinary action.

This principle is also important in developing and maintaining an effective working organization. If the work of the organizational unit is to be carried on in accordance with reasonable standards, the supervisor must, in addition to continually instructing and training employees in the work operations, also counsel and advise them as to their personal work effectiveness.

Every employee, insofar as his or her work is concerned, not only has strong points, but also has weak points. Unfortunately, the supervisor may be all too aware of the deficiencies or weak points of which the employee is unaware or unwilling to acknowledge. Employees are not mind readers. If the shortcomings of the employee are to be corrected or overcome, this action is best facilitated by the supervisor first informing and assisting the employee. Formal performance rating programs, therefore, provide standards and routines for supervisors to counsel employees about work performance, correct situations, and hold employees responsible for improved performance.

Many supervisors fail to carry out this important duty of counseling employees as to how they are performing their work. Employees are frequently permitted to continue working at substandard levels with little attempt by the supervisor to correct the situation or put the responsibility on the employee for improved performance.

Ironically, if the majority of supervisors would carry out this prime responsibilty of regularly appraising the work of their staff and letting them know how things are getting along, there would be no surprises about performance ratings. The daily work effectiveness of each employee would be communicated in such a way that the actual rating would be a formality, a way of documenting for accountability purposes without surprises.

TYPES OF PERFORMANCE APPRAISAL SYSTEMS

Supervisors are fortunate in having different types of appraisal systems available to them. The most widely recognized evaluation practices include checklists and other individual rating scales, narrative assessments, and comparative analyses. Multirater assessments are also being used more frequently in some settings. Choosing which tool or combination of tools to use in conducting employee performance appraisals is based on a variety of factors. However, whether an organization has an established appraisal system or is in the process of creating a new one, knowledge about each of the methods can assist all supervisory managers in understanding and maximizing the effectiveness of the performance appraisal process.

RATING SCALES AND CHECKLISTS

Individual rating scales and checklists present the appraiser with various predetermined personality attributes and/or work-related competencies on which to evaluate the employee. Many of these instruments require scoring an individual's level of performance using numeric scales or selecting the appropriate rating from a range of adjectives such as excellent, good, satisfactory, or unacceptable, which is ultimately converted to a numeric equivalent.

The mean score for all standards represents the employee's overall level of performance.

Checklists generally present objective descriptors of job-related behaviors from which the appraiser chooses those statements that most apply to an individual's performance. In the case of a forced-choice checklist, behaviors are grouped so that each cluster presents several options from which the appraiser must choose only one illustration of the employee's performance. A weighted performance score for the employee is calculated based on the selected items on the checklist.

An example of a predetermined rating scale, in the form of a checklist, follows:

Please rate this employee in each area, according to the following scale: Poor = 0; Fair = 1; Average = 2; Good = 3; Excellent = 4.

___ Job Knowledge

___ Administrative Ability

___ Decision-Making Skills

___ Human Relations Skills

___ Supervisory Ability

___ Communication Skills

___ Initiative

One specific type of rating scale is the behaviorally anchored rating scale, or BARS (Smith & Kendall, 1963). BARS combines the numeric gradations of traditional rating scales with the behavioral descriptors more characteristic of checklists and narratives to create an instrument on which appraisers rate an individual's performance on numerous dimensions, "anchoring" their ratings on observable behaviors. Selected numeric indicators on the scale correspond to clearly defined statements of appropriate behavior for an employee performing at that level. BARS are developed using a complex process that includes identifying, defining, and accurately scaling position-specific behavior statements (Millar, 1990; Pecora & Hunter, 1988).

An example of a BARS approach to the category of job knowledge might appear as follows.

JOB KNOWLEDGE

Behavioral description: measures knowledge of skills, methods, and information relevant to the job and effectiveness in applying that knowledge.

___ 1. Demonstrates insufficient knowledge and skills to do job satisfactorily. Often needs assistance from others in performing daily tasks.

___ 2. Demonstrates sufficient knowledge and skills most of the time. Occasionally needs assistance in performing daily tasks.

___ 3. Demonstrates sufficient knowledge and skills to handle daily activities.

___ 4. Demonstrates thorough knowledge and skills on the job. Requires minimal guidance to handle complex situations. Has good working knowledge of job's relationship to other agency activities.

___ 5. Demonstrates mastery of job knowledge and skills. Is sought after as expert in his/her area. Completely understands how this job fits into the larger organization.

NARRATIVE ASSESSMENTS

Through the use of narrative assessments, appraisers describe the employee's level of performance based on open-ended questions, preestablished criteria, or the documentation of critical incidents. Recording critical incidents (Flanagan, 1949) requires the supervisor to chronicle, throughout the appraisal period, actual events that exemplify various aspects of the employee's performance. These incidents may illustrate positive or negative performance outcomes.

A narrative assessment approach would look something like this:

1. Discuss the employee's strengths and notable accomplishments. Comment on the employee's overall success in achieving the agreed-upon performance objectives.

2. Discuss areas of employee's performance that could be strengthened and improved. Comment on difficulties the employee may have experienced in attempting to achieve performance objectives.

3. Discuss any actions that the employee can take during the next evaluation period to further develop and demonstrate skills and potential on this job.

As described earlier, management by objectives (MBO) is a unique approach to performance appraisal that integrates a specific style of motivating with results-based criteria that can be used as a basis for individual evaluation (Drucker, 1954; Odione, 1965). When using MBO as the basis for a performance appraisal system, the periodic MBO reviews between the managerial supervisor and the employee regarding objective status become performance appraisal systems. As part of this joint review, the managerial supervisor provides the employee with an overall evaluation rating using preestablished guidelines for appropriate levels of objective accomplishment and gives additional feedback on his or her performance in relation to these objectives, which may include critical incident reports or other narrative assessments.

COMPARATIVE ANALYSES

Comparative analyses are another, although somewhat less common, category of evaluation techniques used for performance appraisals. The central tenet of comparative appraisals is the ranking or comparison of one employee's performance in relation to others. Comparison groups may be as small as two, moderately sized (e.g., all employees in the same position or department), or may include all employees within an organization. These comparisons may be open ended or may require a forced choice that ranks all employees according to a normal or bell-curve distribution.

In the example below, a comparative analysis is done on three criteria (i.e., clients seen each day, ratings of that employee by clients, and number of complaints received about that employee). The names of the staff persons would not necessarily be identified, but each person would have a letter I.D. In this way, each employee would know exactly how they compare to their colleagues on the criteria used. See Table 8.1.

Table 8.1: Comparative Performance Analysis

Staff Member	Average Number of Clients Seen Each Day	Average Rating on Client Satisfaction Survey	Number of Complaints Received
A	5	10	0
B	5	5	2
C	4	5	1
D	3	10	0

MULTIRATER ASSESSMENTS

One final type of performance appraisal that merits brief attention is the multirater assessment. Multirater assessments feature more than one appraiser assessing the performance of one employee. One example being used more frequently is the 360-degree feedback process in which the employee, his or her supervisor, peers, staff, clients, and/or other associates evaluate his or her performance using a specified survey instrument (cf. Edwards & Ewen, 1996; Frankel, 1997).

Assessment centers provide a second multirater option. As part of the assessment process, center staff members conduct scored simulations and other skill-based tests to measure employees' performance. These tests provide an opportunity for evaluation-in-action, and results can be used as the basis for performance appraisals.

Examples of the use of each of these evaluation measures can be found among human service organizations. Limited research has been done on the issues arising from the utilization of one form over another. However, there are clearly advantages and disadvantages to each of the performance appraisal systems we have discussed. Rating scales and checklists are easy to complete but tend to rely on vague measurement criteria and supply employees with limited feedback on how to improve their performance. Behaviorally anchored rating scales provide more information to both the appraiser and the appraisee in understanding the meaning of performance ratings; but these are very time consuming to create.

Narrative assessments are more time consuming to complete, but when prepared thoughtfully can provide employees with a more comprehensive appreciation of their strengths and weaknesses and how to improve future performance. The management by objectives approach to performance appraisal holds promise when results-based performance measures are combined with an appropriate level of narrative feedback.

Although comparative assessments may be useful for making personnel decisions, they create the potential for competition among employees. Multirater assessments on the other hand, although more difficult to administer, increase the comprehensiveness of the evaluation, allowing employees to see how their performance affects those with whom they interact, and in the case of skill-based tests, providing an alternative to measure job-related competencies.

THE IMPORTANCE OF INTERACTION

Overall, the effectiveness of performance appraisal systems may be best enhanced by combining several of the techniques described to most accurately measure an employee's level of performance in his or her job. Such systems should be interactive and emphasize employee participation in the appraisal process. This requires that the managerial supervisor and the employee engage in a true dialogue when determining those criteria on which the employee will be evaluated as well as when assessing his or her level of performance. Moreover, every effort should be made to conduct the appraisal in a manner that most completely considers all aspects of the employee's job, builds on his or her strengths, and generates ideas to stimulate career development.

Additionally, there are nine tips that can be offered to supervisors using any and all of the systems we have just described:

1. Be certain employees know how they will be evaluated and have copies of any tools that will be used. This needs to be done when they are first employed, in order to avoid surprises.

2. When meeting with an employee, mention good points first, acknowledging the employee's strengths.

3. Be honest in stating failures and shortcomings that are directly related to job performance.

4. Stick to the facts about shortcomings, giving examples that clearly identify problems.

5. Be careful not to mention shortcomings that do not directly relate to job performance.

6. Recognize that anything that is said is grounded in values, and be careful to recognize unfair value judgments.

7. Put problems in a positive context by suggesting clear ways of improving.

8. Engage in a dialogue, so that the employee has an adequate chance to respond and clarify what has been said.

9. Be careful not to discuss situations beyond the employee's control.

In sum, during performance reviews managerial supervisors must recognize that if a problem is identified, a solution needs to emerge from the interaction. Remember that it is possible to criticize and maintain goodwill. In fact, this is a prerequisite to being a good managerial supervisor. Lastly, every effort should be made to conduct the appraisal in a manner that most completely considers all aspects of the employee's job, builds on his or her strengths, and generates ideas to stimulate career development.

STAFF DEVELOPMENT AND REWARDS

Building on strengths means that managerial supervisors will constantly be looking for ways in which to encourage staff development and provide rewards for employees, particularly when considering that an organization's management approach influences how the human service organization formulates its reward systems. Elements of such systems include salaries, fringe benefits, promotions, and other tangible and intrinsic benefits. This is a challenge, given our earlier discussion of motivation. What is a reward for one person may not be viewed as a reward by another. What is viewed as professional development by one person will be different for others. In other words, a "one size fits all" model cannot be assumed, particularly as workforce diversity increases.

We agree with Tropman (1995) that salaries and the other elements of reward systems can no longer be considered discretely by human service organizations or employees. Rather, akin to the concept of "new pay," base pay must be considered as part of a compensation package that includes all these elements (Tropman, 1995). In addition, this package needs to be based on what the employees want—what they perceive as rewarding.

Dialogue is a critical component here. Managerial supervisors need to talk with staff about what rewards they would like to have and about what they expect.

> For example, the employee who has eagerly embraced advanced technologies and is highly computer proficient may view having the latest computer equipment as a reward, whereas the employee who is still struggling with computer applications may find new equipment intimidating and ultimately overwhelming. The employee who loves to travel and go to conferences will likely feel that a job-based reward is being able to attend a relevant conference, whereas the employee who just wants more time to attend to family needs when she or he is off will see the invitation to attend a conference as a demand on time already stretched too thin. Managerial supervisors must make rewards relevant to the recipient.

Rapp and Poertner (1992) suggest that if an organization is to truly nurture its employees a reward-based environment must be developed. Certainly it is necessary to address problems when they arise, but they suggest that managers have the choice to recognize and reward the positive behavior that occurs within an organization. Rewards need to be immediate and respond to behaviors as they occur: verbal praise should be given by going to the person's work area or calling them to say how much their work is appreciated; written praise may be provided in terms of a personal note, a memo to one's file, a memo to the agency director and newsletter, or even a news release for exceptional work. Symbolic rewards may come in the form of certificates and plaques. Establishing a culture that is reward based becomes easier as positive behaviors and events are shared.

Tropman (1995) suggests four critical steps for organizations moving to new pay reward systems:

1. Fully understand how the existing reward system operates. Successful change is best facilitated when changes can be anticipated.
2. Emphasize continued open and honest communication with employees.
3. Move slowly and incrementally in changing the reward system. You do not have to change everything overnight.
4. Remain flexible in the structure as well as the administration of the system. The ability to adapt to individual and organizational changes is key to the system's success. (p. 1378)

CONCLUSION

As discussed in the beginning of this chapter, the paradox of evaluation occurs at every level within the organization: how to balance the need to motivate with the need to evaluate performance.

To begin to manage this paradox, managerial supervisors must work with agency administrators to create the hiring, motivating, appraising, rewarding, and firing policies and practices that embrace the ideology of the effective organization. It is necessary to inspire confidence and motivation, but that motivation must fit with what is needed to get the work of the organization done. Paradoxically, some employees may be highly motivated, but their energies may be directed toward tasks that do not help the agency get the work done. Managerial supervisors must be skilled at redirecting those energies without reducing employee motivation.

At the same time, human service organizations must address the challenge of how to attract and retain workers who are demanding that their agencies actively support them in their search for meaning and self-actualization (Bolman & Deal, 1995; Handy, 1997; Senge, 1990; Shipka, 1997; Wheatley, 1994). Successful organizations are those in which the individual and the organization as a whole are perceived as productive.

We would consider an effective, competent organization as one that recognizes the value of the work of its employees, but also one in which there is recognition and appreciation of the value of diverse cultural heritages. This is particularly essential in serving diverse client populations.

The managerial supervisor must also be aware that many employees view their workplace almost in the same way as previous generations viewed their local communities—a place that must be meaningful and productive, otherwise why take the risk? How to balance these employee needs in a way that uses the strengths of the workforce is challenging. And since there is no one approach to this challenge, the managerial supervisor will have to be open to change, recognize individual differences, and look for various ways to reward employees who have diverse expectations.

In summary, organizational theorists have over the past century invested a lot of energy in determining the best way to motivate, appraise, and reward agency members. These theories have both influenced and been influenced by several schools of organizational thought. The review of these approaches to practice in this chapter is a reminder that a central paradox exists for managerial supervisors—how to balance the need to motivate with the need to evaluate performance.

9

Protecting Managers as Workers

The previous chapters have all been focused on the role of the managerial supervisor vis-à-vis the needs of their supervisees and/or the needs of the employing organization. In this chapter *we focus on the paradoxical aspects of the role expectations and needs of the managerial supervisors themselves, underscoring the current internal and external realities that place managerial staff at risk in their workplace settings, be they for-profit, nonprofit, or public.*

Many would argue that we are indeed experiencing a system that is out of control as evidenced by the recent downsizing in both the for-profit, the nonprofit, and the public sectors, by at-will dismissals, loss of union protection, outsourcing, the growth in temporary work, and the loss of benefits and pensions. Serious dilemmas are faced by managerial supervisors in these situations. First, while supporting their supervisees in what are often demanding and challenging jobs, they themselves are insecure as management positions are being cut back in a vast array of industries. Second, as workplace conditions of employment are changing, supervisees are also experiencing feelings of insecurity that require attention. Third, in determining what their approach will be to these new circumstances, managerial supervisors must grapple with their roles and responsibilities and the conflict engendered by their concept of professional behavior.

This process is illustrated by several events that transpired in a home health program facing cutbacks. To determine which of the nursing staff would be laid off, all nurses were asked to resign and then required to reapply for their jobs, go through the interview process, and suffer the anxiety of wondering who would stay and who would go. This process served to dismiss those nurses the program did not want to keep (e.g., high salaried professionals, among others) without the risk of a lawsuit. At the same time the agency delayed announcing the decisions, resulting in some persons deciding to leave on their own to take other jobs. And finally, the Human Resources Director, who prepared the dismissed staff for retraining and job searches, was herself dismissed when the department was closed.

Protecting and nurturing the managerial supervisor is the topic we seek to address in this chapter, given the problem of employment instability in the human services. We discuss employment-at-will, whistleblowers, and trade unionism for professionals. We conclude with suggestions for organizational supports of management and staff in this challenging time.

EMPLOYMENT-AT-WILL AND
THE WHISTLEBLOWER

The decade of the 1990s has been one of volatility as industries throughout the nation, including banking, defense, health care, and human services, have been "rightsizing" or "downsizing" to ensure either a balanced budget in the nonprofit and public sectors or a return on investment in the for-profit sector. What has become increasingly used is the "at-will" doctrine in which "the employer maintains the unchallenged power to terminate the relationship at will . . . [predicated on the assumption that] employers need and should be entitled to retain the most qualified personnel without their actions being subject to legal prohibitions" (Tambor, 1995a, p. 46).

Employment-at-will is a doctrine that was developed in response to the industrial revolution in the late nineteenth century and reflects a laissez-faire philosophical view. Wood, in 1877, as discussed in Halbert (1985), articulated the view that employment, for an unspecified period, was a hiring at will, with termination being possible by either the employee or the employer. Thus, for example, the Supreme Court, in its ruling on *Lochner v. New York,* 198 U.S. 45 (1905), ruled that there could be no laws that would control employment conditions and it struck down a state law that required due process for dismissal. The effect of this decision was primarily to protect employer interests.

However, with the change in the political climate of the 1930s, the passage of the National Labor Relations Act placed limitations on this interpretation of contract law. Over the subsequent five decades a series of laws were passed at both the federal and state levels offering workers protection from at-will-dismissals that were based on race, sex, age, or physical handicap. In addition there have been new developments at the state level using contract law principles as well as tort law. Under contract law "there are two main approaches: (1) to find a covenant of 'good faith and fair dealing' implicit in the contract of employment, or (2) to employ a contractual term from the employer's handbook, policy statements or behavior" (Halbert, 1985, pp. 10–11). Under tort law, "courts . . . have been willing to grant a cause of action in tort for wrongful discharge" (Halbert, 1985, p. 15), where an employee has been fired in circumstances that contradict sound public policy. However, both approaches ultimately depend on judgment, and there is much variation by state.

In an earlier decade, Rivas (1984) discussed at-will dismissals from a supervisory and developmental perspective, reflective of concern in that decade with worker's performance. Consequently attention to at-will dismissal was in the context of worker performance, evaluation, and equity of the process, and not cutback management. This illustrates how times have changed; current decisions are based on organizational considerations (i.e., the bottom line, the balanced budget) rather than an individual employee's job performance.

During the past few decades, as society has become more consumer conscious, not only have consumers been mobilized on their own behalf, but some professionals have become "whistle-blowers," concerned with protecting their clients or consumers who were victims of poor professional practice or poorly produced products. Increasing numbers of workers in organizations have begun to make public those problems they witness in the work-place, often with dire and unexpected consequences to them-selves. The protection of whistleblowers is not a foregone con-clusion, and the courts have created narrow exceptions to the at-will doctrine for dismissals (Halbert, 1997). Consequently the approach to whistleblowing is far from clear or consistent.

This is illustrated by the case of a physician who, working for Or-tho Pharmaceutical Corporation, was the only team member to protest clinical tests of a product that the team toxicologist identified as a "slow carcinogen." Ortho dismissed the physician arguing that "as an employee at will, . . . she could be fired for good cause, or bad cause, or no cause at all" (Halbert, 1985, p. 1–2). The New Jersey Supreme Court ruled in favor of the employer contending that the *Food and Drug Administration* had not disapproved the drug, that it was still in the testing phase, and that this was a "difference of medical opinion." The one dissenting opinion stated that the professional au-tonomy of the physician should have been respected and, in line with her professional ethics, she should not have been discharged (Hal-bert, 1985).

The issue of loyalty to the employing organization is often raised in relation to whistleblowing: should employees have a ba-sic responsiblity to the organization that employs them? We agree with the view of Ronald Duska, a director of the Society of Busi-ness Ethics, that the concept of loyalty is not appropriate for an employing organization that is governed either by the profit-making motive or a balanced budget, for there is an inherent con-flict in the situation. The professional is bound by professional ethics irrespective of workplace, and it is the consequence for the consumer that should be the focus.

It may be that whistleblowers in the human services face a dif-ferent situation than those in industry. Specifically, human ser-vice agencies may be more sensitive to public opinion and there-fore may be less ready to force a negative outcome. The following case of a whistleblower in a public sector child welfare agency suggests this possibility, although there certainly are always serious risks involved for the whistleblower.

Big City X was experiencing a dramatic increase in child abuse referrals to The Department of Human Services (DHS) in the early 1980s with cases rising from an average of 2 to 15 a month. These cases were also much more severe than previous ones: more deaths occurred as well as more serious injuries. As a result of these increased problems, the workload of the social workers quadrupled at the same time that the agency was expecting more from the social workers, including more extensive paperwork and more collatoral contacts with neighbors, doctors, and other relevant people—all much more time-consuming activities. Unfortunately these new demands were just not feasible expectations when the numbers of abuse cases were dramatically rising.

Jack Marshall, a young beginning social worker in Child Protective Services, was disturbed by the effects on the children and wrote a letter to all his coworkers suggesting they meet informally to discuss the situation. To his amazement 80 people showed up. Although he was not a public speaker, he made a little speech that, although acknowledging the importance of improving their work, argued that the priority should be getting workers directly into the homes of the abused children, rather than doing the paperwork and other ancillary activities required by the agency.

Marshall made a specific proposal: since the unit had two types of cases, Child Protective Service (CPS) cases, in which abuse had been reported, and General Protective Services (GPS), which dealt with minor problems such as inappropriate dress and breaking curfew, workers should prioritize their work and accept only CPS cases.

The Commissioner rejected this approach because the agency was mandated to deal with children with minor problems as well as children who had been abused. Marshall called another meeting and proposed that if all the social workers refused to take GPS cases, the issue would be forced and they would all be protected since the agency could not fire everyone. Amazingly, all of the workers carried out this action.

The social workers' union informed Marshall that what he was doing was outside of the union contract. If he were a member of the union he would be protected and could not be fired. They offered to support his strategy, and recognizing Marshall's leadership ability, suggested he run for shop steward. A quick election was held and he was made shop steward.

GPS cases piled up and someone informed the state Department of Human Services that there was a union action threatened in Big City X. Fearful of state attention, the Commissioner called an emergency executive staff meeting and suggested that if Marshall could be pushed to an act of insubordination he could be fired and the problem would go away. The strategy was to give him the first GPS case, and if he refused to take it, he would be disciplined. The president of the local union called Marshall to tell him the union would support him and walk out, in support of his action.

Because of the fear of political repurcussions, the Commissioner accepted a compromise. Social workers would accept GPS cases, but would defer additional paperwork on CPS cases. The situation was reported in a series of articles in the local newspaper, a further source of irritation for the Commissioner.

By the late 1980s, many new social workers had been hired to deal with the increasing volume of work and things had stabilized in the Department. Marshall was now an administrator, no longer eligible for union membership. He now reported to the Deputy Commissioner, had a responsible and challenging position in the office of policy and planning, and often worked directly with the Commissioner on special assignments. Their relationship was cordial.

Unexpectedly, a new problem arose: the use of crack had escalated dramatically and many childen died. Every week there was another story about how DHS was not handling these terrible cases. Marshall and other administrators were concerned that the agency was not looking at new approaches needed to deal with the new reality. In fact the Commissioner's response was to ask Marshall to get data that would demonstrate that Big City X was doing no worse than Chicago or Los Angeles. Marshall was appalled and felt that comparisons were not the issue, that the higher rate was the issue, and that the organization was not dealing with the problem. The Commissioner was not providing leadership, the organization was in chaos, workers were frustrated and demoralized, and the State now granted the agency only a provisional license. The only thing that was heartening for the staff was the hope that with the Mayor up for reelection, the Commissioner would be replaced.

This replacement did not happen. Although other Commissioners were replaced, the Commissioner of DHS was reappointed. Furious, Marshall wrote his first letter to the editor as a citizen arguing that the mayor was irresponsible in making this reappointment. As things got worse and nothing happened he wrote a second letter further detailing the situation. The letter was the lead piece on the editorial page along with a caricature of the Commissioner. This now got a response as he received numerous phone calls, many calling him unethical because he worked for the Commissioner. Marshall recognized the risks involved and was very apprehensive because, as a middle manager, he was no longer protected by the union.

In fact there were serious professional consequences to his whistleblowing action. Although he was able to retain both his title and his salary, he was switched from a creative position in the central office to working in a residential off-site facility where he was given a hole-in-the-wall office with nothing to do. Eventually he spoke to the director of that facility and asked for some assignment. The director assigned him to administering the laundry service. Marshall decided he would do all the scut work as best he could and worked in this unfulfilling manner for the next 5 years. With the arrival of a new executive of the off-site facility he was asked to take on the program area since it was clear that Marshall had many creative ideas and his talents were not being utilized.

This whistleblower did pay a price. Why was he not fired? It is probable that the agency did not want to create another public scandal that would bring more public attention to a complex situation.

DILEMMAS SURROUNDING PROTECTIONS

Managerial supervisors are often faced with this dilemma when there is conflict between their professional ethics and their bureaucratic functions. In this time of insecurity few will be willing to serve as whistleblowers and the reality of at-will dismissals is certainly an inhibitor. However, it is urgent that all approaches be considered in seeking to serve clients and consumers effectively.

Given the unclear and uneven public policy at both the federal and state levels, Halbert (1985) makes a powerful argument as she calls for the protection of whistleblowers:

If whistleblowers were able to exercise ultimate control over their employers' practices, surely they would not bother blowing the whistle in the first place. It is far more plausible that they are fired, not because employers were forced to rid themselves of the of-

fending employee before they could act as they saw fit, but as punishment for making waves. . . .

The professional employee . . . should be protected by the common law for expressing concern over, not just a present illegal activity, but a potentially illegal or unethical activity. . . . A cause of
action based on the public policy exception to employment- at-will
should be available to those whose professional code of ethics has
prompted them to blow the whistle. (p. 27)

Tambor (1995a) proposes that arbitration is an appropriate
method for dealing with at-will dismissals and dismissals related
to whistleblowing. This view is based on the assumption that the
situation is negotiable and not just a fait accompli. Gould's (1993)
claim that if the arbitration procedures, which are available in collective bargaining, were used in these cases of at-will dismissals,
as many as 200,000 workers could be reinstated. We question this
assumption since the conditions that lead to at-will dismissals in
our current environment are less related to worker performance
than to organizational interests.

The important factor in this discussion is that managerial supervisors must become knowledgeable and obtain information on
their state laws, as well as federal legislation, in this area. It affects
not only their supervisees but their own job security.

UNIONS IN THE HUMAN SERVICES

The emergence of trade unions as a force in the human services
can be traced to the 1930s when collective bargaining and the
protection of unions became the law of the land with the National
Labor Relations Act of 1935. The major unionization of social
workers took place in the public sector with minimal organization in the private sector. According to Tambor (1995b), the 25%
of the 438,000 social work labor force who are union members
are mainly public sector employees. As the public sector began
extensive contracting with the private sector through purchase of
services in the 1960s and 1970s, support for trade unionism in
the private sector emerged. And in the 1990s organizing efforts
are taking place among health aides and child care workers who
are a critical, but highly underpaid workforce in the human ser-

vices. Their militancy is undoubtedly stimulated by the higher salaries available in for-profit services and the competition for workers in the field.

In the early years of union organizing in the human services many leaders in the social work profession were active proponents of unionism as they believed not only in the improvement of working conditions for social workers but also that social programs would be improved in the process (Galper, 1980). The impetus to organize in the private sector brought with it an added focus on the benefit of participation in agency decision making (Aronson, 1985; DiBicarri, 1985).

The National Labor Relations Act in the 1930s recognized not only the right of employees to organize but also the need to protect workers' interests through the collective bargaining process. As illustrated in Jack Marshall's case, as a union member he was protected; as an administrator he was at risk. Yet, given all the chaos and insecurity in the human services, as discussed in the beginning of this chapter, many managerial supervisors are experiencing role confusion, wondering if they are managers or workers in terms of their feelings of identification and affiliation with the agency versus their expectation of protection by the agency.

This paradox is most apparent when we look at the relationship between managerial supervisors and their supervisees who are union members. It is essential that managerial supervisors fully understand and appreciate the role of the union in the human services, both its positives and negatives, and develop an approach that is fair and respectful. In fact, quite often the issues that are being negotiated have positive spin-off for the professionals in the organization who are not protected by the union. All gain as salaries and benefits are increased and as working conditions are improved.

HOW CAN MANAGERIAL
SUPERVISORS RESPOND?

A bifurcated response on the part of managerial supervisors has been noted in the field. On the one hand many have been union members and bring along their union orientations as they move into administration. On the other hand, others become punitive and rigid in their response to union activity as they move up the organizational ladder, taking the move to unionization as a personal affront. Both of these responses are illustrated in the following situations.

> During a long-term strike, an administrator who had always been an active union supporter went to his office regularly, covered the telephones, and did what was necessary to keep the agency functioning at a minimal level. When asked by his young associate how he dealt with the conflict inherent in the situation, he responded that his role was that of administrator and that the different parties had their own roles to play. There was never any acrimony in his attitude as he met his staff members. This was in sharp contrast to another administrator who was angry, felt betrayed, and developed serious physical symptoms because he personalized the process. (Perlmutter, 1990, p. 16)

In both situations the managerial supervisors were in a new relationship with their former colleagues and peers, one that they were ill prepared to handle, with little training either in making the transition or in handling the new role (Elbow, 1975; Perlmutter, 1990).

In developing an effective approach to working with unions in professional environments it is essential that managerial supervisors recognize that their role carries with it not only many responsibilities but also the need to develop new behaviors and approaches. Our underlying assumption is that managerial supervisors should be respectful, thoughtful, and fair in their response. This requires some homework and preparation. A leader of a local union suggested the following precepts.

First, it is essential that the managerial supervisor understand the contract not only in terms of pay scales, benefits, and working conditions, but also in terms of the implications of the contract on the organization. One way to accomplish this is to work with the Human Resources Department in order to learn what is required and what is left to discretion. There may be more flexibility in the situation than originally seems.

Second, it is essential to remember that cooperation is a two-way street. It is useful to call the union before a situation arises so that the union can be prepared in advance when some action is pending vis-à-vis an employee who is a union member. Courtesy goes a long way and is part of building a relationship between the union and management. All too often management does not consult with or even communicate with the union.

And third, it is essential to remember that management and labor must live with each other for many years. Therefore it is more than a matter of dealing with hard issues; the long-term benefits of a working and mutual give-and-take process are critical for organizational maintenance and health.

MANAGERIAL SUPERVISORS' JOBS: FLOOR OR CEILING?

In addition to the challenges related to whistleblowers and to working with unionization, the managerial supervisor must also cope with an additional stressor on the job. Many managerial supervisors became professional in the ever-expanding environment of the 1960s when the sky was the limit in terms of career possibilities. Thus many human service professionals were socialized to aim for the top and to aspire to continuous opportunities for promotions and career enlargement. Today there is a different reality. Instead of viewing a middle management line as a floor, it now appears to be a ceiling.

Downsizing within organizations is not the only threat to job security people face; they also have to deal with traditional career trajectories being changed as organizations are flattened or merged. In either case, there is less and less opportuniy for moving "up" the ladder. Consequently many managerial supervisors are dealing with their feelings of being in dead-end jobs with little opportunity for personal or professional challenge or recognition. Not only are many experiencing depression and/or burnout, but many are losing a commitment to or an interest in the vitality and health of their employing human service agency.

This emerging fact of life in the human services provides a new challenge in the human resource arena, one identified as critical by an executive of a large nonprofit organization. In his view it is surely incumbent upon central administration to recognize that steps must be taken to energize, recognize, and capitalize on the vast resources that exist in this middle management cohort.

Although it is certainly a challenge for central administration, managerial supervisors must become empowered to identify their own needs and to create opportunities in new ways to find satisfaction, support, and stimulation in the workplace. A first step might be to form peer groups to begin to explore new approaches to a new reality that they themselves can arrange, such as workshops and peer development (Perlmutter, 1983). A major item for the agenda should be to help central administration develop creative forms for recognition of managerial supervisors as well as for job enrichment. One possibility, with powerful potential, is to create a policy advisory group of managerial supervisors that would recognize their expertise and allow them a constructive outlet for their professional competences. In addition to serving an important function for the managerial supervisors, it would also serve organizational interests in valuing these stakeholders and vitalizing their involvement in the agency.

ORGANIZATIONAL SUPPORTS AND DOWNSIZING

The issues addressed in this chapter are complex and painful and we are all attempting to address systemic problems wherein many employees are either at risk or facing job diminishment.

Although the issue of self-interest clearly complicates the matter, managerial supervisors must begin to think about their role as advocates and their potential impact on helping their organizations provide responsible organizational supports in this difficult process. This is not an easy role to play in these circumstances!

A case example from the for-profit sector suggests possible approaches to the problem of downsizing or even closing down.

The Wall Music Inc. was a major retail outfit with 153 stores in 10 states and an annual sales of $160 million. As profits began to fall, The Wall sold its business to a new company and fired 200 employees in the Philadelphia area. This was particularly painful since the store had created a personal family environment for its workers, with a focus on values and commitment to excellence in addition to the profit-making element. The company was committed to making the process as supportive as possible and it adapted the following approaches.

First, the employees were informed of the situation as it developed, with no delayed surprises regarding the closing. Second, from the earliest time, the company helped the employees deal with their emotional response by providing professional help in this process. Third, in addition, the firm conducted many 2-hour training sessions to help the workers in their job search.

Senior management's view was that "the chain had been a model . . . for growth through acquisitions and quickly developing a strong and successful culture. . . . It also should be a model for how to take a company apart when the harsh realities of business say that must be done" ("Company Closes," 1998, p. F1).

Of interest in our discussion is the view of the vice president for store operations that the process "left fewer scars on the managers who had to lay off good employees" ("Company Closes," 1998, p. F12). It must be noted that the motivation on the part of the corporation was not just altruistic: "it provided generous severance payments, help in finding new jobs, and performance bonuses to keep the company strong until the last day" ("Company Closes," 1998, p. F1).

The bottom line of any downsizing program is what ultimately happens to the employee who no longer has a job. However, if the organization can take responsibility for a supportive process, which includes helping with new job referrals and placements, this is a first step.

In addition to these kinds of organizatinal supports for employees, organizations must also be supportive of their managerial supervisors, because the same principles that are important for supervisors to employ with their supervisees in union and downsizing situations are also important to support supervisors facing increasingly complex personal, career, and managment dilemmas in the workplace. Specific attention must be paid to the issues of stress and burnout, which are likely to affect any supervisory manager facing a similarly complex and challenging work environment.

Managerial supervisors are in the unenviable position of being caregivers for the organization, their supervisees, and themselves. Managing these responsibilities means maintaining connections throughout all levels of the organization and caring for many. Kahn (1993) concisely summarizes the effect this can have on the individual. He describes relationships among organizational members as enhancing or reducing individual job performance and suggests that these internal relationships provide a framework for understanding human service and other caregiving organizations. "This frame makes explicit what is implicit in the job burnout literature: The extent to which caregivers are emotionally 'held' within their own organizations is related to their abilities to 'hold' others similarly" (p. 540). Therefore, unless managerial supervisors receive the support they need to care for themselves, they run a great risk of not being able to care for others or for the organization.

Appropriate supports for managerial supervisors would feature an organizational culture that promotes ongoing professional and personal development. For example, such a culture would acknowledge the dilemmas facing managerial supervisors and create opportunities to assist them in developing skills to address them. It would seek out training opportunities and support managerial supervisors in continuing their education in related issues (e.g., dealing with ethical issues within the workplace, working with unions).

A supportive organizational culture would include managerial supervisors in organizational policy setting and direction. It would provide for information sharing and communication throughout the entire organization or among all levels of organizational stakeholders including commissioners or others who help shape organizational decisions. It would offer managerial supervisors the chance to share their concerns and recommendations on a regular basis. Finally, not only would it allow managerial supervisors to be acknowledged for the successes they continue to effect, but it would also allow time for them to relax and feel less pressured.

CONCLUSION

In this chapter we have discussed the increasingly important dilemmas faced by managerial supervisors as they grapple with the various realities incumbent upon their positions. The ultimate challenge is how to balance the tensions experienced between their personal pressures and insecurities with their professional roles and professional ethics. Several approaches can be suggested that can stimulate further thinking in this area. First, it is essential that managerial supervisors become advocates not only for their own supervisees but also for their own cohorts. Second, managerial supervisors must become informed about both the de facto and de jure context of the particular problem or situation, be it whistleblowing or union negotiations, in order to better plan for their response. Third, managerial supervisors must begin to pay serious attention to collaborating with their peers in developing new strategies and approaches to working in these unsupportive realities. Fourth, managerial supervisors must become much more political in their orientations as they seek to broaden their span of influence.

10

Evaluating Program Effectiveness

In the previous chapter we discussed protecting managers in their roles as workers in a complex and changing environment. We now turn to the challenges faced by supervisory managers in protecting the integrity of the programs for which they are accountable. We believe that a program that is accountable must be effective, and that effectiveness means having an impact on the quality of clients' lives, one that they desire. The managerial supervisor plays a critical role in both the implementation and evaluation of the agency's programs.

In this chapter we explore the professional challenges managers face as they encounter several paradoxes related to program effectiveness. First, *although program effectiveness is essential for the achievement of desired outcomes, the evaluation of program effectiveness requires an investment of time and energy from people who are already overworked.* This means that supervisory managers have to recognize that they must nurture their staff and support them in this demanding process.

A second paradox plagues the movement toward outcome measurement and affects all staff levels involved in the process. *If out-*

comes are truly based in quality of life changes for clients, and if those quality of life changes do not conform to what program managers believe they should be, determining appropriate outcomes becomes almost impossible. This poses a vital question that the reflective supervisory manager will have to ask over and over again, "just whose outcome is this anyway?"

We begin this chapter by setting the context within which the supervisory manager can examine the forces that are propelling human service agencies toward outcome-based measurement as a form of accountability. We then highlight what supervisory managers need to know in order to oversee the documentation of program effectiveness through outcome measurement. Given the reality that all contemporary funding sources will reinforce the importance of outcome measurement for program evaluation, it is essential that supervisory managers provide effective leadership in this arena.

THE CONTEXT: THE PUSH
FOR ACCOUNTABILITY

One of the major criticisms of human service programs, both public and private, has been their inefficiency in obtaining effective results. Interest in increased government accountability through outcome measurement can be related to the increased use of government contracting with the private sector to deliver an array of human services. In this relationship a great deal of public money is being spent, but ensuring quality performance of the providers has been elusive. It is difficult to quantify quality of life changes because there are also a broad array of private agencies involved.

Although there have been numerous reform efforts in the public sector such as Planning-Program-Budgeting Systems (PPBS) during the Johnson administration, Management by Objectives (MBO) during the Nixon administration, and Zero-Base Budgeting (ZBB) during the Carter administration, they have not lived up to expectations (Bouckaert, 1990; Affholter, 1994; Mercer, 1992–1993; Hatry, 1992–1993). For example, PPBS, which was designed to prioritize budgeting, resulted instead in burdensome paperwork and calculations so complicated that no one could understand them (Wildavsky, 1964, 1969, 1975).

The interest in program accountability in the public sector continues, shifting some of the action from the federal to the state and local levels. Individual states are beginning to enact their own miniversions of the federal Government Performance and Results Act of 1993, Public Law 103-62, which requires that any program funded with government dollars be outcome based (Kautz, Netting, Huber, Borders, & Davis, 1997). Consequently, outcome measurement, accountability, performance effectiveness, and many other related terms have become part of the human service and social work lexicon (Alsop & McDaniel, 1993; Au, 1996; Auslander, 1996; Kettner, Moroney, & Martin, 1990; Lawlor & Raube, 1995; Netting, Kettner, & McMurtry, 1998; Rapp & Poertner, 1992).

The push for public sector accountability is paralleled in the private nonprofit sector (Bogart, 1995; Chisolm, 1995; Hammack, 1995; Lawry, 1995; Fry, 1995). In the last decade, the press has called attention to those individual nonprofit organizations that have failed to be responsible and accountable for their performance.

For example, "United Way of America is still reeling from revelations about the high salary, perks, and spin-off business opportunities its board afforded to its (former) president" (Hammack, 1995, p. 127). As a result, United Ways are looking for greater accountability and expect their providers to be moving toward outcome-based measurement.

Given this political climate, in which outcome measurement is being toted as the cure-all for program effectiveness in both public and private arenas, the managerial supervisor is placed in the position of overseeing the achievement of these outcomes. Where does a supervisor begin and what are the challenges posed?

CONCEPTUAL ISSUES:
QUALITY AND QUANTITY

How evaluation issues are approached is critical, and all too often managers allow themselves to be seduced by technical experts who focus only on quantitative data. Managerial supervisors have a distinctive contribution to make in this process since they have an understanding of the basic issues to be addressed and the consequences of the decisions.

Grasso and Epstein (1992) encourage the use of a developmental approach to program evaluation, making the point that a major shortcoming of more traditional, after-the-fact evaluations is that what was learned provided little input into program change. They defer to Scriven (1967) who first categorized the differences between summative and formative evaluation. Summative evaluation focuses on retrospection, what happened as a result of the intervention. Formative evaluation is concerned with how things are proceeding along the way. "Following this distinction, developmental evaluation can be defined as a dynamic, future-oriented, applied research approach that uses multiple data sources and research strategies to promote practice and programmatic utilization of findings within direct practice settings" (Grasso & Epstein, 1992, pp. 188–189).

Managerial supervisors, according to Grasso and Epstein, have the responsibility of constantly evaluating both process and outcome and they must convince administration that both are important components in truly understanding program effectiveness. Although funding sources may not always be as interested in the formative aspects of program development as much as in quantitative approaches, it is essential to use mixed methods that combine the best of what is known about qualitative and quantitative data collection, as well as formative and summative approaches.

WHERE TO START IN EVALUATING PROGRAM EFFECTIVENESS?

GETTING STAFF BUY-IN

Given the many changes that are influencing staff in human service agencies today, we have observed that even change agents are resisting change. One day there are layoffs, the next day there is a new information system, and the following week managers are walking around the hallways with a copy of the latest fad in reengineering under their arms. This is not a time in which people feel secure in their positions, and when people are uncertain, there is resistance to change.

However, to truly assess program effectiveness, there is a need to reorient staff members to what this means for their work. No longer is it enough to count outputs (although that is still needed) or even to ask clients if they are satisfied (although that, too, is needed), but now staff members are being asked to focus on the outcomes and impacts of what they do. Outcomes are not as controllable and are harder to measure than are outputs. So, adding this to the workload may not be enthusiastically embraced by everyone.

Supervisory managers, then, must use their best communication and team-building skills to work with staff so that everyone owns the processes that lead to the desired outcomes. This means a lot of face-to-face interaction and hard appraisals of what is expected to happen. It means that staff members see their work as a craft, in which there is an understanding of what happens to a client from beginning to end. This is "owning" the process.

Guterman and Bargal (1996) refer to the client empowerment movement and contend that staff persons cannot possibly think about empowerment of clients if they are feeling disempowered themselves. They discuss the feelings of disempowered staff persons and how these feelings have the potential to affect service outcomes. They point out that staff members who feel that they have lost control in their agency can neither empower clients nor achieve other desired outcomes. They list several strategies that supervisory managers might use in bringing the staff on board under these circumstances:

1. staff development opportunities like advanced training and support for actualizing the special interests and talents of workers;
2. collaborative team-like approach among colleagues;
3. a "safe" organizational environment which allows workers to openly address difficult concerns;
4. a shared organizational philosophy and commitment of the agency;
5. supervisory leadership that communicates support for and positive feedback regarding workers' efforts and that does not critique or obstruct workers' service attempts;

6. administrative "markers" providing recognition and validation of workers' efforts (for example, through promotional opportunities, good salaries, and even comfortable physical working conditions). (p. 15)

The supervisory manager who can promote the factors listed above will likely set a climate in which staff members feel integrated into their programs and who know that their voices will be heard. Their participation in defining desired service outcomes is necessary so that they believe in those objectives.

Designing a Process

Martin and Kettner (1996, p. 21) suggest a link between the social problem to be addressed and the outcome performance measurement to be achieved. Their process includes the following elements, which will help frame our discussion:

1. clarity of the social problem being addressed,
2. an analysis of the underlying assumptions,
3. a clear definition of the human service program,
4. appropriate output performance measures,
5. appropriate quality performance measures,
6. appropriate outcome performance measures.

Knowing What Social Problems Are to Be Addressed

Human service programs are usually designed to address a set of needs within a particular population. Determining what those needs are is sometimes very complicated because different persons will frame the situation in different ways. For example, a program may be said to address homelessness. Although this sounds like a laudable cause, it does not convey much about homelessness or the diversity of the homeless population and its needs.

Once the program manager is hired, she or he will experience a sense of being overwhelmed unless there is more direction than the general mandate to address "homelessness." Specifying what aspects of homelessness will be addressed in this program is critical. This must be followed by targeting a specific subgroup and by setting geographic boundaries. For example, the supervisory manager will find that the program is addressing the problem of homelessness in St. George County and the target population is women and children, or that the target group is older persons who face severe mental health issues. Depending on the target group, the interventions and program design will vary. For working with women and children, social workers with certain skills in child welfare may be needed, whereas if the focus is on older persons with severe mental illness the supervisory manager will look to hire persons with geropsychiatric experience. The problem must be clearly analyzed to fully know how to design the intervention. It is also the responsibility of the supervisory manager to review the literature as the basis for action (see, for example, Kettner et al., 1990).

Identifying Underlying Assumptions

Once the problem has been defined, the supervisory manager must explore the assumptions that underlie the stated problem. As new assumptions are identified it is important to be flexible and open to new ways of framing the original problem. For example, if there are few women and children amid the homeless population in St. George County, then perhaps the assumptions that led to targeting this population need to be reexamined.

Time is limited when a supervisory manager is either setting up a program or is in the middle of implementing a program that has already been in operation for some time. Many supervisory managers inherit their programs and hit the ground running. Taking time to consider the underlying assumptions that led to the program for which they are responsible can be very disconcerting, particularly if they discover that the underlying assumptions were all wrong, but they are committed to that program design since it reflects the views of the different interest groups that have been involved in the process.

Designing the Program

Netting et al. (1998) recommend that the task of understanding a problem requires reviewing the literature on the problem and then focusing on what is known about the target population, collecting supporting data, examining relevant ethnic and gender perspectives on the problem, identifying relevant historical incidents as well as the past experiences of the target population with the problem, identifying barriers to problem resolution, and speculating about the etiology of the problem. This requires supervisory managers to connect with others who have approached these types of problems before. What are other agencies doing? What model programs exist? What does the literature say? Is there research that can inform the intervention?

The significance of program design cannot be underestimated. Kettner et al. (1990) identify three elements of a system: (1) client-related variables, (2) staff-related variables, and (3) physical resources.

Client-related variables include items such as eligibility, demographic or descriptive factors, social history, and assessment of client problem type and severity (Kettner et al., 1990, p. 114). In addition, it is necessary to consider the strengths that clients bring to the program. The supervisory manager must take the opportunity to examine what client inputs are needed.

This step in the process can be illustrated by the following:

A supervisory manager was designing a case management program and the agency administrators were adamant that client outcomes needed to be measured. The team met to determine what outcomes were desired and there was much discussion. Psychiatric social workers were concerned with reducing depression and stress for their clients, whereas registered nurses were particularly concerned about client functioning, which would be greatly enhanced by medication compliance. Other staff members focused on social supports and how important it was to have these in place. The supervisory manager immediately recognized that if depression and stress, functional ability, and social supports were important, there would have to be ways of measuring each of these factors at baseline. Otherwise, no one would ever know if anything had changed. Client inputs, then, included measurement of stress level, depression, functionality, and social support as well as other factors that were identified as relevant to the information collected during client assessment.

In addition, it is important to examine inputs such as what services are used by clients because knowledge on the front end of what clients are using and how those patterns change over time may inform future programming directly linked to client preferences.

Similarly, there are staff-related variables that need to be considered in program design. Kettner et al. (1990) identify demographic or descriptive factors and accreditation factors.

For example, to determine whether African-American staff members are more successful in achieving outcomes with African-American clients than are other staff members, the program has to be designed to track which workers have worked with which clients. If it is considered important to track whether a person has a certain professional degree or educational background, because research has indicated that hiring certain types of staff members is most effective with this clientele, then it is necessary to be sure that these data are collected.

Physical resources are the third element to be considered in designing program evaluations; these include material resources, facilities, and equipment (Kettner et al., 1990). For example, it is necessary to know whether staff members must have computer terminals on their desks or laptops, and what type of office space or vehicles is needed to facilitate the evaluation process.

Ideally, program design means intentionally thinking all of this through before the first client is seen. Based on a careful analysis of the problem and identification of underlying assumptions, the supervisory manager will be able to propose a design that fits with what is known. There is a caveat in this, however. We find that supervisory managers often get excited about the logic of this process and begin to feel comfortable with the way in which one thing leads to another. This is not a linear process and the "logic" of this type of rational approach to program design is seductive. In today's agency, everything is likely to change overnight and all the assumptions once held true about a particular clientele or program can shift. Supervisory managers need to be highly flexible and adaptable and need staff members who can flow with rapid change as well.

Determining Output Performance Measures

Supervisory managers need to know what happens as a result of the efforts made by their staff members in implementing programs. Outputs indicate how many persons are being served, how many hours of service have been completed, and how many new projects have emerged from the program. Outputs are what are produced by the program; by knowing these numbers, a report can be compiled that illustrates what is being produced.

To fully understand outputs the supervisory manager will need to define the units of service that are expected from the program. Martin and Kettner (1996) define a unit of service as "a standardized measure used to determine and report how much service is being provided by a program" (p. 33). Units of service can be "measured in three different ways: (a) an episode or contact unit, (b) a material unit, and (c) a time unit" (p. 33). Episode units are encounters between staff members and clients and are used when it is more important to record contact rather than the specific amount of time spent with a client. A material unit is something tangible such as a check, meal, or voucher given to a client. The time unit, considered to be the most precise of the three types of units of service, is calculated according to the minutes, or partial or whole hours spent with a client. Martin and Kettner (1996) suggest convening a focus group of staff members to determine what units of service are appropriate to measure.

For example, a child welfare program can be measured by several type units of service including material, time, and contact units. Unfortunately the contact unit was not part of the accountability system in one large city where it was found that although the social workers met the requirements of a monthly visit to an at-risk child's home, attention was not paid to the content of the visit and children continued to be abused and even to die in the process.

The supervisory manager is in a position to pursue both the quality and the quantity of the contacts in order to assess what is happening in terms of program performance outputs. If the agency is not paying adequate attention to the content, the supervisory manager must call this to the executive's attention.

Determining Quality Performance Measures

Outputs provide a general picture of program performance. But there are other dimensions that are equally important—what if the meals are delivered, but they taste so bad that clients do not eat them? What if the staff goes into clients' homes, but the persons served feel as if they are not being taken care of well? In other words, what about the quality of what is delivered? There can be very efficient services delivered that have low quality. Conversely, high quality services may be delivered that use so many resources that they cannot be afforded. There must be a balance between quality and efficiency.

The consumer movements and quality management devoted to a focus on quality and excellence in the human services have made great strides in reminding everyone that customer satisfaction is critically important. This is more difficult in some human service agencies that serve persons who do not pay for services or persons who are admitted to the program involuntarily. Consequently there will be managerial supervisors who face a number of constraints in even determining who the actual customer is, much less knowing how to satisfy persons who are required by law to attend (e.g., DUI programs).

Martin and Kettner (1996) identify several dimensions to consider in looking at the quality of human service programs. These include "accessibility, assurance, communication, competency, conformity, courtesy, durability, empathy, humanness, performance, reliability, responsiveness, security, and tangibles" (p. 42). Quality, as defined by the client, is an important concept, and using output performance measures alone is not satisfactory in fully measuring client satisfaction.

Supervisory managers, then, must go beyond determining outputs as measured by calculating units of service. The next step is to determine how the quality of those outputs will be measured. Were clients satisfied with what happened? Supervisory managers can team with staff members to decide just what quality dimensions need to be measured. Will it be accessibility and responsiveness? Can courtesy be assessed? Depending on the program, different quality indicators may be more appropriate. Many programs will opt for developing client satisfaction surveys to obtain the dimensions of quality with which they are concerned. As client satisfaction is becoming more and more important, good survey tools to measure client satisfaction are being developed and implemented all over the country. Having a method to measure satisfaction is becoming an expectation in human service agencies.

Identifying Outcome Performance Measures

By now, the supervisory manager will have worked with staff members to define the problems, to analyze the underlying assumptions of why these problems occur, to design a program intervention that is not only a best guess of how to approach the situation but is flexible as well, to determine what outputs need to be measured, and to find ways to examine the quality of output performance via customer satisfaction. Yet, all of these activities do not ensure an effective program outcome. Supervisory managers must still make sure that outcomes are truly being measured.

Outcomes are defined as quality-of-life changes for clients. This sounds simple enough until an attempt is made to determine what that means to any one individual. Technically, quality of life is a personal thing, and given a healthy respect for diversity, it would be ludicrous to assume that one measure would fit everyone. Yet, that is often the assumption that is made when it comes to determining outcomes.

For example, parents who have been abusive may need rehabilitation. Although giving them parenting classes so that they are more skilled parents may be a socially desirable outcome, a dilemma arises if the parents do not feel the need for these skills. Staff members may feel that teenage mothers have low self-esteem, however, a dilemma arises if the mothers themselves neither feel that they have low self-esteem nor believe that this is an important outcome for them.

Critical to determining quality-of-life changes and their measurements is a healthy sense of skepticism. Certainly, it is important to determine what outcomes will be measured, but it is even more important to have as much input as possible from the persons who will be affected by these changes.

Meaningful indicators are based on the program's goals and objectives; they should cover the breadth of the program's purpose and focus as well as the effects of the program's actions. Human services professionals usually describe outcomes through narratives and anecdotes that favor successful outcomes. Furthermore, narratives focus on those who have been served and do not deal with those people who need the program but are not reached by it. Obtaining valid and reliable qualitative measures is a complex process. For example, interviews of large numbers of program participants require major investments in time and other resources. If the program seeks to expand its interview population to include a control group of those who needed the program but were not participants or clients, the cost multiplies (Kautz et al., 1997).

Since public and private systems seek outcomes in quantitative measures, the managerial supervisor must be challenged to convert the qualitative data collected into quantitative measures. Thus, since many human service programs have records that show quantities of services provided or clients served, managerial supervisors must strive to identify satisfactory quantitative outcome measures that reflect more subtle qualitative information. The use of computerized data facilitates the management and reporting of such measures and it will be a challenge for the managerial supervisor to add to their data banks measures of life changes that have not previously been collected or recorded.

The following example from a large nonprofit agency that serves developmentally disabled persons briefly illustrates some of the steps that were taken by managerial staff to involve staff and administration persons in the evaluation process. In addition, the Board of Directors was included in the process. The case material was prepared by a member of the middle management team.

The disabilities field has undergone a tremendous transformation in the last few decades as public awareness has grown in its appreciation of the abilities and rights of people who are challenged by cognitive or physical limitations. Traditional systems and structures that served "the handicapped" have had to be reoriented to a relationship of partnership in support of individuals with disabilities. Business concepts such as customer service and customer satisfaction are now being applied throughout the human services industry. Changes in design and changes in perspective can be unsettling in any organization, and sweeping change is often more disorienting than refocusing in its effect.

In the recent past, the Community Living and Home Supports program had organized its quality assurance activities in accordance with licensing regulations. Program effectiveness was measured in terms of compliance with established standards. Systematic monitoring of organizational processes and regular reporting up the chain of command were designed to ensure administrators that everyone was adhering to policy and procedure. If problems were identified, plans of correction were developed, then implemented under close supervision. In some ways, "success" came to be defined in terms of the lowest number of problems. Quality was ensured through compliance inspection and evaluation. Quality enhancement was appreciated as an "extra credit"—every once in a while really nice things actually happened to people, and that was fun to celebrate.

When the agency began to evaluate the program's effectiveness in terms of client-based outcomes, systems of inspection and reporting had to be reconsidered and redesigned. A fundamental shift had to occur at the level of the most basic question, "whom do we ask whether or not it's working?" The staff member now asks the customer directly, "Are you satisfied with our services?" and "What do we need to do differently in order to meet your needs and expectations?" Case managers and licensing inspectors still monitor the agency's licensed programs, but feedback on the quality-of-life indicators is now part of the process. Questions are being asked such as do people choose their daily routine, and do people choose where and with whom they live?

These are certainly new questions based on the assumption that some information can be obtained from the clients themselves and that customer satisfaction and quality of life are more important than the rigid adherence to professional routines. Consequently, expectations of staff members are changing now that customer satisfaction and quality of life are core indicators of organizational effectiveness. Staff members who directly support people with disabilities play a critical role in evaluating the effectiveness of the organization's effort.

Former traditional systems of evaluation and inspection did not prepare staff members for these new roles. As they worked under constant inspection, they felt they had little power, autonomy, or authority and consequently did not see themselves as accountable to their clients. Instead they were more likely to consider clients as the objects of their daily work, and themselves as next-to-the-bottom level of the proverbial food chain.

The managerial supervisors, in making this shift, have had to pay careful attention to each staff person's developing sense of strength and worth as they redesign the organization's system of accountability. Everyone is held accountable to the needs and satisfaction of the customers, staff persons participate in the evaluation of their managerial supervisor's effectiveness, and everyone is included and represented when task forces, committees, and improvement teams are formed. Thus, person-centered thinking that focuses on the consumer is explored and encouraged throughout the program.

The work of Community Living and Home Supports did not arise from a self-determined initiative of the people who receive or purchase the services of the organization. Rather, it was seen as an opportunity market by the administration of a large social service organization. The work was consistent with the agency's stated mission and their sincere interest in serving their community. Initial perspectives on program effectiveness were focused on compliance with regulatory authorities and fiscal integrity. As the agency became an established stakeholder in the Mental Health and Mental Retardation (MH/MR) system, its leaders recognized that the organization's integrity required a focus on accountability to the people who are supported by its services. Embracing a movement sweeping across the disabilities field, they concentrated on the goal of satisfying each customer, and worked to improve quality of life as each client determines that to be. Staff members have regularly kept the board informed of the developments in the field and have brought the needs of the community to their attention.

Members of the agency's board have also accepted a level of accountability to the community by regularly visiting individuals in the program. The needs and concerns raised by board members are addressed by staff members, who are in turn accountable to the board. Several members of the board are taking advocacy roles in the wider sociopolitical arenas, and staff members will be supporting these efforts as well.

CONCLUSION

The implementation of outcome measurement is a major contribution to be made by the managerial supervisor who be-

comes the linchpin in the process—a person who fully understands the processes leading to various outcomes and who can
articulate those processes to the various participants who
must be involved. This includes staff persons, as discussed
above, as well as administration. It may seem strange that we
would suggest that one of the challenges for the supervisory
manager is to get the administration of the organization on
board, but that is exactly what we are suggesting. Although administrators will be pushing for outcome measurement in the
programs for which their agencies are accountable, they will
not necessarily have the time to examine in detail every outcome measurement decision that is made. This translator role
is critical to the organization's understanding of its program
and its effectiveness.

The push toward accountability in human service organizations and the need to evaluate the effectiveness of their programs have come from multiple directions in the past decade.
The supervisory manager can expect this trend to continue at
a rapid pace.

To assess program effectiveness, managers can begin by determining what problems are to be addressed by their programs and
what underlying assumptions are brought to bear on these problems. Once program directions are agreed upon, it will be
important to determine output performance measures, quality
performance measures (client satisfaction), and outcome performance measures. All three types of measures are important and
each tells a different story about what is happening. In the case
of the Community Living and Supports Program presented above,
a program staff person familiar with output performance had to
be oriented to both quality performance and outcome performance measures. This required telling their story from a more
client-centered perspective. It also meant translating program outcomes for Board members.

The managerial supervisor is indeed a linchpin in the
agency: he or she must serve as a leader for staff members
as they participate in the evaluation process, a translator
of what program outcomes mean to administration, and an

educator to the Board of Directors so that it can understand and be committed to the process. This linchpin role clearly places the managerial supervisor in a pivotal position in the agency in advocating for a developmental approach to program evaluation.

EPILOGUE
WHERE DO WE GO FROM HERE?

THE challenges faced by managerial supervisors have been the focus of this book. In this final discussion we link these challenges with opportunities, to underscore the reality that what we do can make a difference. The metaphor of the managerial supervisor as the leader of a jazz band suggests not only the diverse and exciting elements of this performance but also the interdependent relationship between the band leader and the members that enhances everyone's performance.

Our discussion has often been framed around paradoxes currently faced in the field. It is the existence of these competing truths that provides room for professionals to exercise their best judgment.

> The constraints created by ambiguous mandates can be viewed as an opportunity since they leave the executive room for decision-making and action; since the signals are unclear, there is greater lattitude for individual interpretation. This is a state to be desired by a risk-taker who can use this lack of clarity to press for unorthodox options and alternatives. (Perlmutter, 1980, p. 60)

We have aimed in this book to support and encourage the exercise of professional judgment and creativity. Professional effectiveness rests not only on one's creativity but as well on an under-standing and analysis of each challenging situation. It also requires recognition of the effects of the potential solution on multiple con-stituencies. As this book has affirmed, this complex understanding is particularly urgent when, as is often the case, there is no absolute or clearcut solution to a professional challenge.

In this epilogue we will suggest positive responses through ex-amples related to the chapters in this volume. As noted earlier, the intent is not to provide solutions or recipes for behavior, but rather to stimulate a broader repertoire for analysis and response.

MEETING PROFESSIONAL CHALLENGES
FOR MANAGERIAL SUPERVISORS

In our opening chapter we identified the paradoxes, and chal-lenges, created by ideological, economic, social, and technologi-cal changes in today's turbulent environments. The mix of providers from the nonprofit, for-profit, and public sectors con-tinues to add a complex dimension to the challenge. The stres-sors created by all these environmental elements make it clear that it is no longer business as usual. What may become usual is the necessity for social service administrators to initiate and im-plement meaningful change at an increasingly rapid pace and with a new organizational arrangement.

An example of an innovative response stimulated by manager-ial supervisors was the development of a program by a local fam-ily agency to serve the families of HIV patients when the larger community was not yet ready to acknowledge the existence of AIDS. The program was initiated by managerial supervisors who, recognizing the pressures on the family members and the stigma and shame they were experiencing, explored the possibility of a new program with the Executive Director of a new service that would support these people. The Executive Director agreed and received the approval of the Board of Directors.

The new program included the critical element of advocacy as a need surfaced that was not acceptable in the public's percep-tion. The program identified new professional roles that chal-lenged traditional services and stimulated the development of new relationships among the public, for-profit, and nonprofit sectors. The agency became a model on a state-wide basis and served to stimulate the initiation of similar programs in other settings. This example clearly illustrates the opportunity for managerial supervisors to influence responsive organizational program development.

RESPONDING TO LEGAL MANDATES

In our complex and litigious society, it is essential that managerial supervisors not only be informed about the laws that directly relate to their supervisees but also that they be flexible and adaptive in responding to these legal challenges. For example, the societal response to legislation regarding sexual harassment in the workplace has been mixed. There has been confusion about developing appropriate organizational arrangements to deal with the law, and attitudes within the organization have often been complex, conflict producing, and gender based.

Our discussion of this topic highlighted a group of managerial supervisors in a large public bureaucracy who recognized that havoc was being generated among staff members by the rigid structure created by central administration. They decided not to wait until after the first case came to the fore, but rather to begin a multidimensional staff development process. They recognized that it was important for their staff members to understand the organizational expectations and to be clear about the procedures, but that it was equally important to handle the reactions to this new requirement. To handle the less tangible element, they decided to have discussions with groups by gender, as a first step, and then to follow these up with discussions involving mixed groups of workers.

This indeed was proactive thinking and served to pave the way for a healthy organizational climate to evolve in preparation for handling the cases that came to the fore. This was in sharp contrast to the hostility that surfaced in a sister organization in a neighboring county that did not anticipate the problem and did not seek a solution until much anxiety and conflict was engendered.

BUILDING STRATEGIC ALLIANCES

A paradox of competition and collaboration can arise whenever organizations form strategic alliances. Just as persons are responsible for the agencies in which they are employed and these agencies are often competitive with others, human service organizations are finding themselves increasingly committed to alliances that require principles and behaviors that are collaborative in nature, but competitive in details.

The case of Maria Rodriguez and the Elder Care Management Program illustrates the primary structures used by organizations that participate in an alliance, be it an affiliation, a federation/ association, or even a joint venture or consolidation. After highlighting the major reasons underlying strategic alliances, we explore the areas of knowledge, skills, and values critical to supervisory managers in overseeing an alliance. The Elder Care case also serves to identify the eight key components of an alliance and to study their interactions during formation and development of the alliance.

In the present environment, in which forces of competition and collaboration coexist, effective supervisors must learn how to manage these competing demands. To do so, managers need to be able to discern both the costs and benefits of alliance building. Recognizing the reality of the demands of competition and collaboration enables supervisors to be most effective in this work.

HUMANIZING TECHNOLOGY

Recognition of technological changes in the workplace leads to a recognition of how all encompassing the term "technology" can be; it can refer to all the tools used to communicate (e.g., telephones, faxes, computers) as well as to the skills used by the practitioner to provide good service (from cognitive restructuring to community organizing). To guide managerial supervisors in obtaining a better grasp of the technological change within their organizations, we focused on the importance of identifying supervisees' needs in order to effectively communicate with one another and with consumers of service.

We followed a managerial supervisor through the array of possibilities encountered in information systems and recognized the very human response of being overwhelmed when faced with the challenges of new hardware and software. To be user friendly, we tried to break the process down somewhat, so that the manager would know where to begin. We encouraged the managerial supervisor to ask relevant questions and affirmed the fact that if someone does not understand how a system "works," then professional problem-solving skills can be used to resolve the situation.

The managerial supervisor interacts with both the system designers and line staff, playing both a linkage and a translator role. This very human approach can support staff development in the era of computerization. Managerial supervisors can develop policies that reflect the use of new technologies and nurture staff members in the process of recognizing what technologies can do for them.

On a positive note, it should be pointed out that the potential for staff members in human service organizations to use E-mail, the web, and the Internet opens a new world of possibilities to accessing information quickly from their own desks. For example, advocacy efforts can be magnified through electronic mailing lists, with information on a bill that affects human service clients reaching thousands of interested persons in minutes! The managerial supervisor who seizes the opportunity to fully assess and access technological options will be riding the wave of the future.

FACILITATING COMMUNICATION

Just as the chapter on humanizing technology focused on linking persons to one another electronically, our chapter on facilitating communication continued the dialogue. We underscored the significance of communication as the glue that holds the human service enterprise together. Without good communication, the system literally breaks down.

We provided an assessment guide for managerial supervisors in this chapter, beginning with in-person communication— formal and informal, verbal and nonverbal. We looked at telephone and voicemail, using an example of a large multipurpose human service agency in which there were so many steps to access a "real" voice that consumers were irate, and justifiably so.

The potential misunderstanding that can arise from written communication was illustrated when a managerial supervisor communicated to staff that he wanted to "invite" them to a meeting and every person on the task force interpreted this "invitation" differently. This illustration emphasizes what we consider to be the most important message in this chapter—that no matter how clear people think they are being, they should expect to be misunderstood. Using that basic principle enables professionals to expect miscommunication, and therefore not to take it personally when miscommunication occurs.

Regarding cross-cultural and gender issues in communication, current demands will create more and more opportunities for managerial supervisors to work with persons from diverse backgrounds. Strategies for effective communication include how to confront conflict, how to use strategic talk, and how to be clear in written messages. These very interpersonal skills will increasingly be in demand, even more so in an age of technology. What we discovered as we examined the professional management literature is that everyone emphasized the importance of good communication. Not only has this need increased, but as people communicate in so many different ways, the savvy managerial supervisor will be the person who has insight into how communication works, why it breaks down, and how to reconnect the estranged parties.

SUPPORTING DIVERSITY

The expectation of diversity in organizational life (e.g., gender, ethnicity, age, race, and religion) is a reality that is here to stay. To address the critical work found in effective diversity programs, the paradox of uniqueness and similarity through a sociopolitical perspective suggests that managerial supervisors must first understand their own views and behaviors toward diversity in order to facilitate the creation of the "empathetic self" in themselves and in their staff, and within the organization's systems and policies.

At the personal level, the empathetic self requires recognition of both the ways in which we are similar and the ways in which we are interdependent with one another. Although seemingly a very simple process, managers must know that such work requires patience and tolerance for ambiguity and frustration in themselves and their staff. At the organizational level, responding to changing diverse employees and client groups necessitates revisiting service provision and system-wide policies and practices.

Several typologies have been offered for recognizing an organization's need for training in diversity. An approach is detailed for using mixed member or intergroup dialogues for diversity implementation.

CREATING AND SUSTAINING INTERDISCIPLINARY TEAMS

The reality of differences and similarities that was examined in the chapter on diversity is also an important element in forming and maintaining interdisciplinary teams. Just as staff members must be competent, autonomous professionals trained in their respective disciplines, so must they simultaneously function well in teams that are interdependent and mutually beneficial, demanding reciprocity in meeting members' interests, orientations, and needs. This duality highlights one of the paradoxes inherent in the human services.

A definition and elaboration of interdisciplinary teaming are provided by a case example of a long-term care rehabilitation team that is used to explore the complex responsibilities inherent in team leadership. The focus in this discussion is on team leadership, which we view as the keystone for the formation and maintenance of an effective team experience. The approach is very applications oriented as it highlights critical components that can inform the team leader's strategy in forming and managing effective interdisciplinary teams.

Exploring the paradox of relationship inherent in these teams affords supervisors several ways to begin to manage this issue while also acknowledging that some teams are actually dysfunctional and therefore require specific interventions. To differentiate between functional and dysfunctional teams and to optimize the benefits of all, we believe that supervisory managers must fully understand both the pros and cons of teaming. Examining the benefits and costs underscores the need for managerial supervisors to be skillful in supporting their individual team members while concurrently attending to the members' departments and the organization at large.

MOTIVATING, APPRAISING, AND REWARDING

For many supervisors, two of the most challenging fundamental areas of management are (1) how to motivate employees to perform at their best in the best interest of the agency and (2) how to evaluate employees' performance from the personal and organizational perspective. There are two inherent paradoxes in this area. First, how can the supervisory manager balance the need to motivate with the need to evaluate performance? Second, how can this manager balance the individual motivators of employees with the agency's culture and needs?

This paradox related to performance evaluation provides the central thesis of this chapter. This work examines the evolution of managerial beliefs and actions from the early 1900s to the present. Following this overview, several major theories on motivation are identified. The supervisor is faced with the challenge of determining how to manage his or her employees so as to assist them in doing their best in their current jobs while providing a good foundation for future growth and development.

With this as a base, samples of the most commonly used performance appraisal and reward systems are presented. These systems are described and examples are provided to guide the manager in creating an evaluation environment that is most supportive of the employee. The central message is that the management of the evaluation process is ongoing, and that continuous interaction and effective communication between managerial supervisors and their staff members are necessary for success.

PROTECTING MANAGERS AS WORKERS

Managerial supervisors often struggle with being close to both front line staff and administrative leadership in the organization. Although they may identify with front line issues, their managerial positions require that they respond in a manner that considers the total organization's needs. Among the various critical aspects, they must consider matters such as employment-at-will and the whistleblower, professional unions in the human services, and the challenges of managing downsizing.

It is essential that some emotional distance be created between one's professional and one's personal responses to the competing and contradictory demands that create a paradoxical challenge. This is best illustrated by the responses of two different administrators to a similar circumstance. Both were in unionized settings and there was much stress in the workplace as a strike was called for the professional staffs in each agency. The executive of one agency felt under seige and became hostile and combative, believing that he had been betrayed by a staff whom he had always protected and cared for. He even developed an ulcer during the union negotiations. By contrast the executive of the second agency viewed the strike as one alternative approach of the union; he separated his personal feelings (which were actually prounion) from his ability to see the strikers as playing their roles while he played his. His major focus was to keep in perspective that they would all be working together after the strike was settled and, therefore, that a major concern was to be respectful and civil during this difficult and demanding process in order to ensure positive relationships for the future.

The thorny issues of worker protection, and the conflicts experienced by the managerial supervisors, are challenges for these professionals, who must simultaneously deal with their own needs while meeting organizational requirements. In an unstable environment this is not a simple process.

EVALUATING PROGRAM EFFECTIVENESS

In an age of outcome measurement, it was very important to emphasize program effectiveness and the push for greater accountability that is occurring on all fronts. Keeping the evaluation of program effectiveness in mind, managerial supervisors must consider the various elements needed to fully link a social problem addressed by their agencies to measurable performance indicators. A helpful example focuses on the homeless and the complex needs of this diverse population. In this case the managerial supervisors worked with homeless women and children, a subgroup of the larger homeless population.

An even more comprehensive program described in the text looked at a large nonprofit agency serving developmentally disabled persons. When the agency began to evaluate program effectiveness in terms of client-centered outcomes, its systems of inspection and reporting had to be reconsidered and redesigned. A fundamental shift had to occur to the level of the most basic question, "whom do we ask whether or not this program is working?" The point is that outcome measurement can be meaningful only if the outcomes are quality-of-life changes that clients truly want to have happen. As the managers in this system began to recognize the strengths of various constituencies, diverse voices could be heard in the push for system integrity and accountability.

We are encouraged by the push toward more effective programming, and we believe managerial supervisors are well positioned to hear what consumers and line staff are telling them about what is important to measure. Managerial supervisors who can design evaluation systems for their programs that truly reflect quality-of-life changes for consumers will be in great demand.

A FINAL NOTE

An underlying assumption of this book, and one stated throughout, is that managerial supervisors are a critical cohort in the human service delivery system. They link the policy-governance and administrative arm of the agency with front line realities.

This epilogue focuses attention to one potential contribution that this group can make, not discussed earlier, that demands the most adventurous, creative, and even outrageous explorations. Such an outreach requires developing a futurist perspective that projects into the near future (i.e., 5–15 years) and the far future (i.e., 15 years and beyond).

A futurist perspective provides a positive context that goes past the immediate realities and its constraints to long-range visions of what is desirable. This view is shared by a growing movement of academicians and professionals who are exploring long-range issues, as illustrated by the development of the World Future Society. Although much of the activity is theoretical and academic, the implication for professionals in the human services who are more reality oriented is the potential for making possible in the future what has not yet been achieved in the present.

Macarov (1991) points out that all too often human service professionals are reticent to become involved in efforts for social change. Yet, he suggests, a future orientation coupled with a sensitivity to the needs of the client community provides a handle in working for social change as it forces professionals to think about long-range possibilities. Managerial supervisors can bring to the fore special opportunities for their organizations, if, in anticipating the future, they are able to take new approaches as they seek to fulfill their organizations' mission.

The unique perspectives, both present and future, place the managerial supervisor in a critical position vis-à-vis the political process. Given the interrelationship between public policy and private needs, who is better positioned to provide testimony, to advocate for, and to work with people and communities at risk?

And finally, the exciting thing about managerial supervision is that there is much to learn and many opportunities for creative and stimulating work. Our view is that education for effective performance should be an ongoing process and that professionals should take advantage of continuing education, professional conferences, and professional books and journals that are increasingly focused on management of the human services.

References

Adams, J. S. (1965). Inequity in social exchange. In L. Berkowitz (Ed.), *Advances in experimental and social psychology*, Vol. 2 (pp. 267–300). New York: Academic Press.

Adelman, C. (1997, July/August). Diversity: Walk the walk and drop the talk. *Change*, 34–45.

Affholter, D. P. (1994). Outcome monitoring. In J. S. Wholey, H. P. Hatry, & K. E. Newcomer (Eds.), *Handbook of practical program evaluation* (pp. 96–112). San Francisco: Jossey-Bass.

Albrecht, L., & Brewer, R. M. (Eds.) (1990). *Bridges of power: Women's multicultural alliances*. Philadelphia: New Society Publishers.

Alderfer, C. P. (1972). *Existence, relatedness, and growth: Human needs in organizational settings*. New York: Free Press.

Allen-Meares, P., & Lane, B. A. (1990). Social work practice: Integrating qualitative and quantitative data collection techniques. *Social Work, 35*(5), 452–458.

Alsop, R., & McDaniel, N. (Eds.) (1993, March). *Proceedings of the first national roundtable on outcome measures in child welfare services*. San Antonio, TX.

Amey-Taylor, M. (1998). *Diversity trainers: Personal profiles, paradigms, and practices*. Unpublished doctoral dissertation. Temple University, Philadelphia.

Aronson, R. L. (1985). Unionism among professional employees in the private sector. *Industrial and Labor Relations Review, 38*, 352–364.

Au, C. (1996). Rethinking organizational effectiveness: Theoretical and methodological issues in the study of organizational effectiveness for social welfare organizations. *Administration in Social Work, 20*(4), 1–21.

Auslander, G. (1996). Outcome evaluation in host organizations: A research agenda. *Administration in Social Work, 20*(2), 15–27.

Auslander, G. K., & Cohen, M. E. (1992). Issues in the development of social work information systems: The case of hospital social work departments. *Administration in Social Work, 16*(2), 73–88.

Bailey, D. (1991). Designing and sustaining effective organizational teams. In R. L. Edwards and J. A. Yankey (Eds.), *Skills for effective human services management* (pp. 142–154). Silver Spring, MD: NASW Press.

Bailey, D., & Koney, K. M. (1995). Community-based consortia: One model for creation and development. *Journal of Community Practice, 2*(1), 21–41.

Bailey, D., & Koney, K. M. (1996). Interorganizational community-based collaboratives: A strategic response to shape the social work agenda. *Social Work, 41*(6), 602–611.

Bailey, D., & Koney, K. M. (2000). *Creating and maintaining strategic alliances: From affiliations to consolidations.* Thousand Oaks, CA: Sage.

Ballard, Spahr, Andrews, & Ingersoll. (1997). *Employment & Labor Law Seminar* (handouts).

Barzelay, A., & Armajani, B. J. (1992). *Breaking through bureaucracy: A new vision for managing in government.* Berkeley, CA: University of California Press.

Bass, B. (1990). From transactional to transformational leadership: Learning to share the vision. *Organizational Dynamics, 18*(3), 19–31.

Bennis, W. G., & Shepard, H. A. (1961). Group observation. In W. G. Bennis, K. D. Benne, & R. Chin (Eds.), *The planning of change* (pp. 743–756). New York: Holt, Rinehart & Winston.

Berger, P. L., & Luckman, T. (1967). *The social constructing of reality.* Garden City, NY: Anchor.

Bion, W. (1959). *Experiences in groups.* New York: Basic Books.

Bogart, W. T. (1995). Accountability and nonprofit organizations: An economic perspective. *Nonprofit Management and Leadership, 6*(2), 157–170.

Bolman, L. G., & Deal, T. E. (1995). *Leading with soul.* San Francisco: Jossey-Bass.

Bouckaert, G. (1990). The history of the productivity movement. *Public Productivity and Management Review, 14*, 53–89.

Bray, C. (1995). Defining workplace abuse. *Affilia, 10*(1), 87–91.

Brown University. (1986). *The American University and the pluralist ideal: A report of the Visiting Committee on Minority Life and Education at Brown University.* Newport, RI: Brown University Press.

Brown, A., & Bourne, I. (1996). *The social work supervisor.* Buckingham, England: Open University Press.

Bryant, A. (1998). Quest for fire: Looking for purpose in a paycheck. *New York Times, Week in Review,* section 4, p. 1.

Bulin, J. G. (1995). *Supervision: Skills for managing work and leading people.* Boston: Houghton Mifflin.

Burgdorf, R. L., Jr. (1991). The Americans with Disabilities Act: Analysis and implications of a second-generation civil rights statute. *Harvard Civil Rights-Civil Liberties Law Review, 26*, 413–522.

Caputo, R. K. (1986). The role of information systems in evaluation research. *Administration in Social Work, 10*(1), 67–77.

Champagne, D. (1997). Does the focus on multiculturalism emphasize differences and foster racial/ethnic stereotypes? Yes. In D. de Anda (Ed.), *Controversial issues in multiculturalism* (pp. 27–33). Boston: Allyn & Bacon.

Chatterjee, P. (1998). Consultation. The Mandel School of Social Work, Case Western Reserve University, Cleveland, OH.

Chisolm, L. B. (1995). Accountability of nonprofit organizations and those who control them: The legal framework. *Nonprofit Management and Leadership, 6*(2), 141–156.

Clark, P. G. (1997). Values in health care professional socialization: Implications for geriatric education in interdisciplinary teamwork. *The Gerontologist, 37*(4), 441–451.

Cleveland, J. N., & Shore, L. M. (1996). Work and employment. In J. E. Birren (Ed.), *Encyclopedia of gerontology: Age, aging & the aged* (pp. 627–639) San Diego, CA: Academic Press.

Comerford, S. A. (1998). *Learning through engaging—engaging through learning: Towards a contextualist, relational approach to adult learning about diversity.* Unpublished doctoral dissertation. Weatherhead School of Management, Department of Organizational Behavior, Case Western Reserve University, Cleveland, OH.

Company closes, but aids workers through changes. (1998 March 30) *Philadelphia Inquirer*, pp. F1, F12.

Cox, T. (1994). *Cultural diversity in organizations.* San Francisco: Berrett-Koehler.

Cross, T. (1988). Services to minority populations: Cultural competence continuum. *Focal Point, 3*(1), 1–4.

Dart, J. W., Jr. (1993). Introduction: The ADA: A promise to be kept. In L. O. Gostin & H. A. Beyer (Eds.), *Implementing the Americans with Disabilities Act: Rights and responsibilities of all Americans* (pp. xxi–xxvii). Baltimore: Paul H. Brookes.

Decker, B. (1988). *The art of communication: Achieving interpersonal impact in business.* Oakville, Canada: Reid Publishing Ltd.

dePree, M. (1992). *Jazz leadership.* New York: Dell.

Dezendorf, P. (1997). Privatization: Private problem or public issue? *Social Work Executive*, pp. 1, 5, 7.

DiBicarri, E. (1985). Organizing in the Massachusetts purchase of service system. *Catalyst, 5*(17–18), 45–50.

Dreher, D. (1996). *The Tao of personal leadership.* New York: Harper Business.

Drinka, T. J. K., & Streim, J. E. (1994). Case studies from purgatory: Maladaptive behavior within geriatric health care teams. *The Gerontologist, 34*(4), 541–547.

Drucker, P. F. (1954). *The practice of management.* New York: Harper.

Drucker, P. F. (1992). *Managing for the future: 1990s and beyond.* New York: Truman Talley Books/Dutton.

Drucker, P. F. (1995). *Managing in a time of great change.* New York: Truman Talley Books/Dutton.

Eden, D. (1988). Pygmalion, goal setting, and expectancy: Compatible ways to boost productivity. *Academy of Management Review, 13,* 639–652.

Edwards, M. R., & Ewen, A. J. (1996). How to manage performance and pay with 360-degree feedback. *Compensation and Benefits Review, 28,* 41–46.

Edwards, R. L., & Reid, W. J. (1989). Structured case recording in child welfare: An assessment of social workers' reactions. *Social Work, 34*(1), 49–52.

Elbow, M. (1975). On becoming an agency executive. *Social Casework, 56,* 525–530.

Emery, F. E., & Trist, E. L. (1969). The causal texture of organizational environments. In F. D. Emery (Ed.), *Systems thinking* (pp. 241–257) New York: Penguin.

Equity Institute. (1990, June). *Renewing commitment to diversity in the 90s.* Paper presented at the 16th Annual Nonprofit Management Conference, Cleveland, OH.

Etzioni, A. (1993). *The Spirit of community.* New York: Crown.

Fabricant, M. (1985). The industrialization of social work. *Social Work, 30*(5), 389–395.

Fatout, M., & Rose, S. R. (1995). *Task groups in the social services.* Thousand Oaks, CA: Sage.

Fiedler, F. E. (1967). *A theory of leadership effectiveness.* New York: McGraw-Hill.

Fisher, R., & Karger, H. J. (1997). *Social work and community in a private world: Getting out in public.* White Plains, NY: Longman.

Flanagan, J. C. (1949). A new approach to evaluating personnel. *Personnel, 26,* 35–42.

Fox, Rothschild, O'Brien, & Frankel. (1996). *Labor & Employment Law Seminar* (handouts).

Frankel, L. P. (1997). Using 360-degree feedback instruments: Holding up the mirror. *Employment Relations Today, 24,* 37–50.

Friedman, J. J., & Ditomaso, N. (1996). Myths about diversity: What managers need to know about changes in the U.S. labor force. *California Management Review, 38*(4), 54–77.

Fry, R. E. (1995). Accountability in organizational life: Problem or opportunity for nonprofits? *Nonprofit Management and Leadership, 6*(2), 181–195.

Gallos, J. V., Ramsey, V. J., & Associates. (1997). *Teaching diversity: Listening to the soul, speaking from the heart.* San Francisco: Jossey-Bass.

Galper, J. (1980). *Social work practice: a radical perspective.* Englewood Cliffs, NJ: Prentice Hall.

Gant, L. M. (1996). Are culturally sophisticated agencies better workplaces for social work staff and administrators? *Social Work, 41*(2), 163–171.

Gant, L. M., & Guitierrez, L. M. (1996). Effects of culturally sophisticated agencies on Latino workers. *Social Work, 41*(6), 624–631.

Gibelman, M., Gelman, S. R., & Pollack, D. (1997). The credibility of nonprofit boards: A View from the 1990s and beyond. *Administration in Social Work, 21*(2),21–40.

Gibelman, M. & Kraft, S. (1996). Advocacy as a core agency program: Planning considerations for voluntary human service agencies. *Administration in Social Work, 20*(4), 43–59.

Goldman, H. (1997). Interview. Jewish Family and Children Service. Philadelphia.

Gould, W. (1993). *Agenda for reform.* Cambridge, MA: MIT Press.

Grasso, A. J., & Epstein, I. (1992). Toward a developmental approach to program evaluation. *Administration in Social Work, 16*(3/4), 187–203.

Gray, B., & Wood, D. J. (1991). Collaborative alliances: Moving from practice to theory. *Journal of Applied Behavioral Science, 27*(1), 3–22.

Griessman, B. E. (1993). *Diversity: Challenges and opportunities.* New York: Harper Collins.

Guitierrez, L. M. (1992). Empowering ethnic minorities in the twenty-first century: The role of human service organizations. In Y. Hasenfeld (Ed.), *Human services as complex organizations* (pp. 320–338). Newbury Park, CA: Sage.

Gummer, B. (1995). Go team go! The growing importance of teamwork in organizational life. *Administration in Social Work, 19*(4),85–100.

Gummer, B. (1997). Heads it's no: Current perspectives on strategic decision making. *Administration in Social Work, 21*(1), 73–90.

Gummer, B. (1998). Current perspectives on diversity in the workforce: How diverse is diverse? *Administration in Social Work, 22*(1), 83–100.

Guterman, N. B., & Bargal, D. (1996). Social workers' perceptions of their power and service outcomes. *Administration in Social Work, 20*(3), 1–20.

Hackman, J. R. (Ed.) (1990). *Groups that work (and those that don't)*. San Francisco: Jossey-Bass.

Halbert, T. A. (1985). The cost of scruples: A call for common law protection for the professional whistleblower. *Nova Law Journal 10*(1), 1–27.

Halbert, T. A. (1997). *Law and ethics in the business environment*. Minneapolis/St. Paul, MN: West.

Hammack, D. C. (1995). Accountability and nonprofit organizations: A historical perspective. *Nonprofit Management and Leadership, 6*(2), 127–139.

Hammer, M. (1996). *Beyond reengineering*. New York: Harper Business.

Handy, C. (1994). *The age of paradox*. Boston: Harvard Business School Press.

Handy, C. (1997). *The hungry spirit*. New York: Broadway Books.

Hasenfeld, Y. (1983). *Human service organizations*. Englewood Cliffs, NJ: Prentice Hall.

Hatry, H. (1992–1993). The alphabet soup approach. *The Public Manager, 21*, 9.

Haynes, K. S. (1989). *Women managers in human services*. New York: Springer.

Henton, D., Melville, R., & Walesh, K. (1997). *Grassroots leaders for a new economy: How civic leaders are building prosperous communities*. San Francisco: Jossey-Bass.

Herzberg, F., Mausner, B., & Snyderman, B. B. (1959). *The motivation to work*. New York: Wiley.

Heyman, R. (1994). *Why didn't you say that in the first place? How to be understood at work*. San Francisco: Jossey-Bass.

Hirschhorn, L. (1991). *Managing in the new team environment*. Reading, MA: Addison-Wesley.

Hochberger, J. M., & Wheelan, S. A. (1996). Assessing the functional level of rehabilitation teams and facilitating team development. *Rehabilitation Nursing, 21*(2), 75–81.

Hoefer, R. A., Hoefer, R. M., & Tobias, R. A. (1994). Geographic information systems and human services. *Journal of Community Practice, 1*(3), 113–127.

Holland, T. P. (1976). Information and decision making in human services. *Adminstration in Mental Health, 4*(1), 26–35.

Holloway, S., & Brager, G. (1989). *Supervising in the human services: The politics of practice*. New York: Free Press.

Huber, R., Borders, K., Netting, F. E., & Kautz, J. R. (1997). To empower with meaningful data: Lessons learned in building an alliance between researchers and long-term care ombudsmen. *Journal of Community Practice, 4*(4), 81–101.

Jarman-Rhode, L., Mcfall, J., Kolar, P., & Strom, G. (1997). The changing context of social work practice: Implications and recommendations for social work education. *Journal of Social Work Education, 33*(1), 29–46.

Johnston, W. B., & Packer, A. E. (1987). *Workforce 2000: Work and workers for the twenty-first century.* Indianapolis, IN: Hudson Institute.

Jones, A. & May, J. (1992). *Working in human service organizations.* Melbourne, Australia: Longman Cheshire.

Kadushin, A. (1992). *Supervision in Social Work.* New York: Columbia University Press.

Kagle, J. D. (1993). Record keeping: Directions for the 1990's. *Social Work, 38*(2), 190–196.

Kahn, W. A. (1993). Caring fo the caregivers: Patterns of organizational caregiving. *Administrative Science Quarterly, 38*(4), 539–563.

Katzenbach, J. R., & Smith, D. K. (1993). *The wisdom of teams.* New York: McKinsey.

Kautz, J. R., Netting, F. E., Huber, R., Borders, K., & Davis, T. S. (1997). The government performance and results act of 1993: Implications for social work practice. *Social Work, 42*(4), 364–373.

Kettner, P. M., Moroney, R. M., & Martin, L. L. (1990). *Designing and managing programs: An effectiveness-based approach.* Newbury Park, CA: Sage.

Kolb, D. A. (1985). *Learning-Style Inventory* (rev. ed.). Boston: McBer.

Kotter, J., & Heskett, J. (1992). *Corporate culture and performance.* New York: Free Press.

Kramer, R. M. (1981). *Voluntary agencies in the welfare state.* Los Angeles: University of California Press.

Kreuger, L. W. (1997). The end of social work. *Journal of Social Work Education, 3*(1), 19–27.

Lakey, B., Lakey, G., Napier, R., & Robinson, J. (1995). *Grassroots and nonprofit leadership: A guide for organizations in changing times.* Philadelphia: New Society.

Lakoff, G., & Johnson, M. (1980). *Metaphors we live by.* Chicago: University of Chicago Press.

Lawlor, E. F., & Raube, K. (1995). Social interventions and outcomes in medical effectiveness research. *Social Service Review, 69*(3), 383–404.

Lawry, R. P. (1995). Accountability and nonprofit organizations: An ethical perspective. *Nonprofit Management and Leadership, 6*(2), 171–180.

Learning-Style Inventory: A manual for teachers and trainers. Boston: McBer.

Locke, E. A., & Latham, G. P. (1990). *A theory of goal setting and task performance.* Englewood Cliffs, NJ: Prentice Hall.

Lohmann, R. A. (1992). *The commons: New perspectives on nonprofit organizations and voluntary action.* San Francisco: Jossey-Bass.

Love, A. J. (1990). Internal evaluation: Building organizations from within. *Applied Social Research Methods Series,* Vol. 24. Newbury Park, CA: Sage.

Luszki, M. B. (1958). *Interdisciplinary team research: Methods and problems.* New York: National Training Laboratories by New York University Press.

Macarov, D. (1991). *Certain change: Social work practice in the future.* Silver Spring, MD: NASW.

Martin, L. L., & Kettner, P. M. (1996). *Measuring the performance of human service programs.* Thousand Oaks, CA: Sage.

Maslow, A. (1943). A theory of human motivation. *Psychological Review, 50,* 370–396.

Maslow, A. (1954). *Motivational personality.* New York: Harper & Row.

McClelland, D. (1961). *The achieving society.* Princeton, NJ: Van Nostrand.

McConkey, D. D. (1975). *MBO for nonprofit organizations.* New York: McGraw-Hill.

McCready, D. J., Pierce, S., Rahn, S. L., & Were, K. (1996). Third generation information systems: Integrating costs and outcomes. Tools for professional development. *Administration in Social Work, 20*(1), 1–15.

McGregor, D. (1960). *The human side of enterprise.* New York: McGraw-Hill.

McGregor, D. (1967). *The professional manager.* New York: McGraw-Hill.

McMurtry, S. L., Netting, F. E., & Kettner, P. M. (1990). Critical inputs and strategic choice in nonprofit human service agencies. *Administration in Social Work, 14*(3), 67–82

Menefee, D. (1997). Strategic administration of nonprofit human service organizations: A model for executive success in turbulent times. *Administration in Social Work, 21*(2), 1–19.

Mercer, J. (Winter 1992–1993). GPRA. *The Public Manager, 21,* 17.

Millar, K. I. (1990). Performance appraisal of professional social workers. *Administration in Social Work, 14*(1), 65–85.

Miller, J. B. (1991). The development of women's sense of self. In J. V. Jordan, A. G. Kaplan, J. B. Miller, I. A. Stiver, & J. L. Surrey (Eds.), *Women's growth in connection* (pp. 11–26). New York: Guilford Press.

Mizrahi, T., & Rosenthal, B. (1993). Managing dynamic tensions in social change coalitions. In T. Mizrahi & J. Morrison (Eds.), *Community organization and social administration: Advances, trends, and emerging principles* (pp. 11– 40). New York: Haworth Press.

Morgan, G. (1997). *Images of organization.* Thousand Oaks, CA: Sage.

Muller, H. J., & Parham, P. A. (1998). Integrating workforce diversity into the business school curriculum: An experiment. *Journal of Management Education, 22*(2), 122–148.

Murphy, J. W., & Pardeck, J. T. (1992). Computerization and the dehumanization of social services. *Administration in Social Work, 16*(2), 61–72.

Myers, S., Jr. (1997, July/August). Why diversity is a smoke screen for affirmative action. *Change,* 25–32.

Nadler, D. A., & Lawler, E. E., III. (1997). Motivation: A diagnostic approach. In J. R. Hackman, E. E. Lawler, III, & L. W. Porters (Eds.), *Perspectives on behaviors in organizations* (pp. 26–38). New York: McGraw-Hill.

Nagda, B. A., Spearmon, M., Holley, L. C., Harding, S., Balassone, M. L., Moise-Swanson, D., & de Mello, S. (1997, November). *Intergroup dialogue, education and action: Innovation in a school of social work.* Paper presented at the conference on Intergroup Dialogue, Ann Arbor, MI.

National Assembly of National Voluntary Health and Social Welfare Organizations. (1991). *The community collaboration manual.* Washington, DC: Author.

Netting, F. E., & Williams, F. E. (1996). Case manager-physician collaboration: Implications for professional identity, roles and relationships. *Health and Social Work, 21*(3), 216–224.

Netting, F. E., Kettner, P. M., & McMurtry, S. L. (1998). *Social work macro practice,* 2nd ed. New York: Longman.

New York Times, April 30, 1997, pp. A1, D22.

Nhat Hanh, T. (1995). *Living Buddha, Living Christ.* New York: Riverhead Books.

Odiorne, G. S. (1965). *Management decision by objective.* Englewood Cliffs, NJ: Prentice Hall.

Ostrander, S. A. (1989). Private social services: Obstacles to the welfare state? *Nonprofit and Voluntary Sector Quarterly, 18*(1), 25–45.

Pacanowsky, M. (1995). Team tools for wicked problems. *Organizational Dynamics, 23*(3), 20–35.

Parker, G. M. (1990). *Team players and teamwork: The new competitive business strategy.* San Francisco: Jossey-Bass.

Pecora, P. J., & Hunter, J. (1988). Performance appraisal in child welfare: Comparing the MBO and BARS methods. *Administration in Social Work, 12*(1), 55–72.

Perlman, S., & Bush, B. H. (1996). Fund-raising regulation: A state-by-state handbook of registration forms, requirements and procedures. New York: Wiley.

Perlmutter, F. D. (1980). The executive bind. In F. D. Perlmutter & S. Slavin (Eds.), *Leadership in social administration* (pp. 53–71). Philadelphia: Temple University Press.

Perlmutter, F. D. (1983). Caught in between: The middle management bind. *Administration in Social Work, 8*(1), 147–161.

Perlmutter, F. D. (1987). Administration: External aspects. In A. Minahan (Ed.-in-Chief), *Encyclopedia of social work*, 18th ed. Silver Spring, MD: NASW.

Perlmutter, F. D. (1990). *Changing hats: From social work practice to administration.* Washington, DC: NASW.

Perlmutter, F. D. (1997). *From welfare to work: Corporate initiatives and welfare reform.* New York: Oxford University Press.

Perlmutter, F. D., & Adams, C. T. (1990). The voluntary sector and for-profit ventures. *Administration in Social Work, 14*(1), 1–14.

Perlmutter, F. D., & Adams, C. T. (1994). Family service executives in a hostile environment. *Families in Society, 75*(7), 439–446.

Peters, T. (1987). *Thriving on chaos.* New York: Harper & Row.

Peters, T. (1992). *Liberation Management.* New York: Knopf.

Rapp, C. A., & Poertner, J. (1992). *Social administration: A client centered approach.* White Plains, NY: Longman.

Reich, R. (1992). *The work of nations.* New York: Vintage Books.

Richan, W. C. (1980). The administrator as advocate. In F. D. Perlmutter & S. Slavin (Eds.), *Leadership in social administration* (pp. 72–85). Philadelphia: Temple University Press.

Rivas, R. F. (1984). Perspectives on dismissal as a management prerogative in social service organizations. *Administration in Social Work, 8*(4), 77–92.

Roberts-DeGennaro, M. (1986). Factors contributing to coalition maintenance. *Journal of Sociology and Social Welfare, 13*(2), 248–264.

Roberts-DeGannaro, M. (1997). Conceptual framework of coalitions in an organizational context. *Journal of Community Practice, 4*(1), 91–107.

Rock, B. D., Beckerman, A., Auerbach, C., Cohen, C., Goldstein, M., & Quitkin, E. (1995). Management of alternative level of care patients using a computerized database. *Health & Social Work, 20*(2), 133–139.

Root, L. S. (1996). Computer conferencing in a decentralized program:

An occupational social work example. *Administration in Social Work*, *20*(1), 31–45.

Rosenthal, B. B., & Mizrahi, T. (1990, Spring). Coalitions: Building strength from diversity. *NY Ragtimes* (pp. 1, 3, 4). New York: Regional Association of Grantmakers.

Salzburg Seminar. (November 15–22, 1997). Working Group C. Cooperation and Partnership: The interface of NGOs with public and private sector actors. Session 351: Non-Governmental Organizations: Leadership and Civil Society. Salzburg, Austria.

Sashkin, M. (1995). Visionary leadership. In J. Thomas Wren (Ed.), *The leader's companion: Insights on leadership through the ages* (pp. 402–407). New York: The Free Press.

Schein, E. H. (1985). *Organizational culture and leadership.* San Francisco: Jossey-Bass.

Schein, E. H. (1992). *Organizational culture and leadership,* 2nd ed. San Francisco: Jossey-Bass.

Schindler-Rainman, E. (1988). Team building in voluntary organizations. In W. B. Reddy with K. Jamison (Ed.), *Team building: Blueprints for productivity and satisfaction* (pp. 119–123). Alexandria, VA: NTL Institute for Applied Behavorial Science.

Schopler, J. H., & Galinsky, M. J. (1995). Group practice overview. *Encyclopedia of Social Work,* 19th ed. (pp. 1129–1142). Washington, DC: NASW.

Schutz, W. (1966). *The interpersonal underworld.* Palo Alto, CA: Science and Behavior Books.

Scott, W. E., Jr., Farh, J. B., & Podsakoff, P. M. (1988). The effects of "intrinsic" and "extrinsic" reinforcement contingencies on task behavior. *Organizational Behavior and Human Decision Processes, 41,* 405–425.

Scriven, M. (1967). *The methodology of evaluation.* In R. W. Tyler, R. M. Gagne, & M. Scriven (Eds.), *Perspectives of curriculum evaluation.* AERA Monograph Series on Curriculum Evaluation, No. 1. Chicago: Rand McNally.

Semke, J. I., & Nurius, P. S. (1991). Information structure, information technology, and the human services organizational environment. *Social Work, 36*(4), 353–358.

Senge, P. M. (1990). *The fifth discipline.* New York: Doubleday.

Shaffer, C., & Anudsen, K. (1993). *Creating community anywhere.* Los Angeles: Tarcher/Perigee.

Sheets, T. L., & Bushardt, S. C. (1994). Effects of the applicant's gender-appropriateness and qualifications and rater self-monitoring propensities on hiring decisions. *Public Personnel Management, 23*(3), 373–382.

Shera, W., & Page, J. (1995). Creating more effective human service organizations through strategies of empowerment. *Administration in Social Work, 19*(4), 1–15.

Shipka, B. J. (1997). *Leadership in a challenging world: A sacred journey.* Newton, MA: Butterworth-Heinemann.

Shulman, A. D. (1996). Putting group information technology in its place: Communication and good work group performance. In S. R. Clegg, C. Hardy, & W. R. Nord (Eds.), *Handbook of organization studies* (pp. 355–374). Thousand Oaks, CA: Sage.

Shulman, L. (1992). *Interactional supervision.* Washington, DC: NASW.

Silberman, H. (1990). *Active Training.* New York: Lexington Books.

Slavin, S. (1980). A theoretical framework for social administration. In F. D. Perlmutter & S. Slavin (Eds.), *Leadership in Social Administration* (pp. 3–21). Philadelphia: Temple University Press.

Smith, D. M., & Kolb, D. A. (1986). *User's guide for the Learning-Style Inventory: A manual for teachers and trainers.* Boston: McBer.

Smith, P. C., & Kendall, L. M. (1963). Retranslation of expectations: An approach to the construction of unambiguous anchors for rating scales. *Journal of Applied Psychology, 47,* 149–155.

Steckler, N., & Fondas, N. (1995). Building team effectiveness: A diagnostic tool. *Organizational Dynamics, 23*(3), 20–35.

Stern, M. (1984). The politics of American social welfare. In F. D. Perlmutter (Ed.), *Human services at risk* (pp. 3–22). Lexington, MA: Lexington Books.

Synergos Institute (1992). *Holding together: Collaborations and partnerships in the real world.* New York: Author.

Tambor, M. (1995a). Employment-at-will or just cause: The right choice. *Administration in Social Work, 19*(3), 45–57.

Tambor, M. (1995b). Unions. *Encyclopedia of social work,* 19th ed. (pp. 2418–2426). Washington, DC: NASW.

Tannen, D. (1990). *You just don't understand.* New York: William Morrow.

Tannen, D. (1994). *Talking from 9 to 5 women and men in the workplace: Language, sex and power.* New York: Avon Books.

Taylor, F. W. (1911). *Principles of scientific management.* New York: Harper.

The Slade Company Case. (1960). Boston: President and Fellows of Harvard College.

Thomas, D. A., and Ely, R. J. (1996). Making differences matter: A new paradigm for managing diversity. *Harvard Business Review, 74*(5),79–90.

Thomas, D. A., & Wetlaufer, S. (1997). A question of color: A debate on race in the U. S. workplace. *Harvard Business Review, 75*(5), 118–132.

Thomas, K., & Velthouse, B. (1990). Cognitive elements of empowerment: An "interpretive" model of intrinsic task motivation. *Academy of Management Review, 15*(4), 666–681.

Thomas, R. (1996). *Redefining diversity.* New York: AMACOM.

Thomas, R. (1998). Diversity in community. In F. Hesselbein, M. Goldsmith, R. Beckhard, & R. Schubert (Eds.), *The Community of the Future* (pp. 71–81). San Francisco: Jossey-Bass.

Thomas, R. R. (1991). *Beyond race and gender: Unleashing the power of your total work force by managing diversity.* New York: American Management Association.

Trickett, E. J., Watts, R. J., & Birman, D. (1993). *Human diversity: Perspectives on people in context.* San Francisco: Jossey-Bass.

Tropman, J. E. (1995). Strategic pay/new pay. In J. G. Maurer, J. M. Shulman, M. L. Ruwe, & R. C. Becherer (Eds.), *Encyclopedia of Business,* Vol. 2. (pp. 1376–1378). Detroit, MI: Gale Research.

Tuchman, B. W., & Jensen, M. A. C. (1977). Stages in small group development revisited. *Group and Organization Studies, 2,* 419–427.

U. S. Equal Opportunity Commission, BK 17, 1991.

Vaill, P. B. (1991). *Managing as a performing art: New ideas for a world of chaotic change.* San Francisco: Jossey-Bass.

Vinokur-Kaplan, D. (1994). Integrating work team effectiveness with social work practice: An ecological approach. In D. Tucker, R.C. Sarri, & C. Garvin (Eds.), *The integration of social work and social science.* Westport, CT: Greenwood Press.

Waldfogel, J. (1997). The new wave of service integration. *Social Service Review, 71*(3), 463–484.

Walster, E., Walster, W., & Berscheid, E. (1978). *Equity: Theory and research.* Boston: Allyn & Bacon.

Webster's seventh new collegiate dictionary. (1965). Springfield, MA: G. & C. Merriam.

Weirich, T. W. (1980). The design of information systems. In F. D. Perlmutter & S. Slavin (Eds.), *Leadership in social administration* (pp. 142–156). Philadelphia: Temple University Press.

Wheatley, M. J. (1994). *Leadership and the new science.* San Francisco: Berrett-Koehler.

Wheelan, S. (1994). *Group processes: A developmental perspective.* Needham Heights, MA: Allyn & Bacon.

Wildavsky, A. (1964). *The politics of the budgetary process.* Boston: Little, Brown.

Wildavsky, A. (1969, March/April). Rescuing policy analysis from PPBS. *Public Administration Review, 29,* 189–202.

Wildavsky, A. (1975). *Budgeting: A comparative theory of budgetary processes.* Boston: Little, Brown.

Williams, F. G., Netting, F. E., & Engstrom, K. M. (1991, Winter). Implementing computer information systems for hospital-based case management. *Hospital and Services Administration, 36*(4), 559–569.

Young, D. R., Bania, N., & Bailey, D. (1996). Structure and accountability: A study of national nonprofit associations. *Nonprofit Management and Leadership, 6*(4), 347–365.

Zeff, R. (1996). *The nonprofit guide to the internet.* New York: Wiley.

Zuniga, M. (1997). Does the focus on multiculturalism emphasize differences and foster racial/ethnic stereotypes? No. In D. de Anda (Ed.), *Controversial issues in multiculturalism* (pp. 35–39). Boston: Allyn & Bacon.

Index

About the Authors

Felice Davidson Perlmutter, PhD, is Professor and Chair of the Administration/Planning Concentration in Temple University's School of Social Administration. A former Fulbright Scholar, she has extensive experience as a teacher, consultant and researcher on a national and international level. She teaches in the areas of administration, social policy, and supervision/staff development. Dr. Perlmutter is an active contributor to the nonprofit and social work literature. She serves on numerous boards of directors on the local and national level.

Darlyne Bailey, PhD, is Dean and Professor at the Mandel School of Applied Social Sciences at Case Western Reserve University in Cleveland, Ohio. She holds a secondary appointment in the Weatherhead School of Management and chairs the governing body of the Mandel Center for Nonprofit Organizations. Dr. Bailey is currently a board member of the Council on Social Work Education, a Group XIII Fellow in the W. K. Kellogg National Leadership Program, and past co-chair of the National Organizational Behavior Teaching Society Board.

F. Ellen Netting, PhD, is Professor of Social Work at Virginia Commonwealth University. Dr. Netting has taught courses in policy practice, administration and planning, and gerontology and is an active researcher in these areas. Dr. Netting's numerous publications include books and articles in her areas of special interest: nonprofit management and service delivery issues in aging. She is active on many professional boards in gerontology, nonprofit organizations, and social work.